From the Street

to the CROSS

The Devil Is a Liar, God Is Truth

Misty Kinzel

From the Street to the Cross
The Devil Is a Liar, God Is Truth
by Misty Kinzel

Printed in the United States of America.

ISBN 9781498462327

The names and places in the book have been changed to protect the privacy of all involved, but the events are all true.

www.xulonpress.com

Dedication

I want to dedicate my story to God for never leaving my side. Also to my dad, Charles Edward Kinzel III, Charlie Buvel, Ruth Irick, Joe Irick Sr., Richard Irick, Grandma and Grandpa, Aunt Susie, Aunt Debbie, Aunt Kathy, Uncle Junior, Uncle Dave, and my three beautiful kids, Travis Irick, Trey Irick, and Demytria Hunt for never giving up on me and believing in me.

Table of Contents

Table of Contents

Acknowledgments

I would like to thank Dr. Larry Keefauver and Pam McLaughlin for their help in putting this manuscript together into book form so I could share my story and my message with others. I would also like to thank Lynn Brewer, from the Human Trafficking Coalition, and also Isevelt "Izzy" and Marshawna Laquerre for encouraging me to do motivational speaking and finishing this book that I had started ten years ago. I know I could not have done it without all of you!

Introduction

Mustard Seed Faith

Jesus *(pointing to a nearby mulberry tree)*: *It's not like you need a huge amount of faith.* If you just had faith the size of a single, tiny mustard seed, you could say to this huge tree, "Pull up your roots and replant yourself in the sea," and it would *fly through the sky and* do what you said. *So even a little faith can accomplish the seemingly impossible.* (Luke 17:6 VOICE)

My name is Misty Kinzel and I want to tell my story in the hopes it will help those who feel they are out of hope and think they have nowhere else to turn but the street or an abusive relationship. I am living proof God is there for every single one of us.

I have lived a very unfortunate life, but I do not want people who read this book to feel sorry for me. I want these stories to give them hope that no matter what they have experienced in life, God is there for them.

I did not grow up in a home where we went to church or read the Bible. All I remember as far as any kind of reference to God was when my mother gave me a necklace with a little tiny seed in it. She said all I needed was faith the size of that little mustard seed to be able to pray and ask God for help whenever I was in trouble. I truly wish I had understood what that meant and put it into practice as I walked through the next thirty years of my life. One thing I do know, God was always there even though I was not aware of it at the time. Now I want to share what I have learned with you!

God has said, "Never will I leave you; never will I forsake you." (Hebrews 13:5 NIV)

Chapter 1

Stolen Innocence

But whoever causes one of these little ones who believe in and acknowledge and cleave to Me to stumble and sin [that is, who entices him or hinders him in right conduct or thought], it would be better (more expedient and profitable or advantageous) for him to have a great millstone fastened around his neck and to be sunk in the depth of the sea. (Matthew 18:6 AMP)

All my life I have fought the demon of sexual abuse and the fact that no one would believe me when I finally told them what was being done to me. This abuse and treatment from my family ate away at my very soul and pushed me down a destructive path in life. Keeping all the hurt, shame, and abuse inside gave me this unloved, empty feeling. Later, my street name was "Gankster," but it really should have been "Lost and Misunderstood." Things started happening to me at a very young age.

I actually do not remember too much about my childhood other than I spent a lot of time staying with my aunt and uncle before I was of school age. I also remember how much I loved my grandfather. He collected and flew model airplanes. He was so much fun to be around until he got real sick with leukemia and passed away. I remember missing him a lot. My grandmother was always amazing as well. She made the most wonderful banana bread. It makes my mouth water just to think about it!

My mom came from a household of seven girls who lived in a small, two bedroom, one bathroom house. That is probably why she married her first husband very young. He died of an overdose and then she married her second husband, my dad, who named me his Misty Lynne after the movie, "Play Misty for Me." Unfortunately, for both of us, he was an abusive man and beat her so she finally left him and married my step-father who is actually the man who raised me from the age of three. He and my mom were married for twenty-five years until he died peacefully in his favorite reclining rocking chair. Later, mom married the mailman. Out of my mother's first marriage, I have an older half-sister and an older half-brother.

When I was about five or six years old, both of my parents worked and my stepsister, who was nine years older than me, would sneak boys into the house and hide them in the closet until my parents went to work. Then my stepbrother, and I would leave for school. Once we went back and looked in the window to see her apparently having sex with one of these boys, though I did not know what was going on at the time. However, I would soon find out that my brother knew exactly what was going on.

At first my stepsister and I were very close. She would tell me how much she loved me and was so glad I was her little sister. However, when my mother would notice and ask her where she got the bruises on her neck and arms, she blamed me. When I was then punished for something I did not do, I began to not trust or believe what my "loving" stepsister said.

About this time my stepbrother, who was five years older than me, decided to start sexually abusing me. I remember I would often come home from school and be so tired I would put a pillow over my head and fall fast asleep. My sister always told me I was a very deep sleeper and nothing would wake me up once I was fully asleep. Apparently my brother figured this out as well and used it to his advantage.

When I woke up I would be partially undressed, but I did not remember undressing before I fell asleep. At first, I did not really pay too much attention to it, but when it continued to happen more and more, I decided to see if something was happening while I was asleep. I put the pillow over my head and pretended to be asleep. My stepbrother came into my room and carefully pulled down my pants and underwear and started touching me. I jumped up and asked him what he was doing. He said he was just curious and for me not to tell anyone. Things escalated from there as we began to explore one another's bodies. From there my stepbrother decided to teach me about oral sex.

He would announce at dinner that he had some new records he wanted me to listen to. So after dinner, we would go to his room, he would put the music on loud enough to cover any sounds we made, and he would force me into oral sex. This happened every night.

When my stepsister was sixteen, she married her boyfriend. I liked him, and I fooled around a lot. He would tickle me and say he thought it was fun to be with me. Then he started telling me I was beautiful and he loved me a lot. He said one day he would leave my sister and marry me. After my sister gave birth to my nephew, she needed help so I stayed with her and her husband. One day, when she was asleep in the next room, her husband told me to come over on the couch with him, he wanted to tickle me. Later, I realized what he was calling tickling was really oral sex. I did not understand it at the time, though, and actually thought it made me feel good.

I liked his attention, and he kept telling me how much fun I was and how beautiful I was and how much he loved me. However, then he would tell me I must never tell anyone about our tickling. That was to be our little secret. By the time I was eleven, my brother-in-law moved us into full blown sex and took my virginity. From then on we would have sex three or four times a week whenever we could hide from my sister. This went on for years. I really did not think there was anything wrong with this because he said he loved me. He was my whole world.

Is this Really Love?

My girlfriend and I loved to watch the movie Grease. One day her dad was home and came into join us. He lay down on the bed with us and began to touch us telling us it was just like in the movie. Then he too escalated and wanted to do a lot more than just touch. In fact, growing up, the only man that did not touch me or have me engage in some form of oral sex was my step-father. I thought he did not do any of this to me because he didn't love me when in fact he was the only one that really did. He was one of the few men in my life that really did love me!

One day I walked into another of my girlfriend's house and saw her father having sex with her in the shower. She looked at me with such a pleading look, like make him stop that I began to wonder if all of this was right or not. He seemed embarrassed that I walked in on them and would never go after her if I was there. So I started going there more and more often to help protect her from him. I learned later that she eventually killed her father and wound up in jail.

Then when I was twelve, they held a sex education class in my school. When I realized what they were talking about was how my stepbrother, my girlfriend's father, and my brother-in-law were treating me, I knew for sure this was not right. I went right to my brother-in-law and told him I was not going to let him touch me ever again. He stopped, but told me he would hurt me bad if I ever told anyone what had happened between us.

I told my stepbrother I was not going to go to his room and "listen to records" any more with him either. He told me he would beat me up if I didn't do what he told me to do. The very next time I did what he wanted, I left his room and ran away that very night for fear of what would happen to me if I refused to do everything he wanted.

With all this going on in my life, I started drinking and smoking pot. The drugs and alcohol helped me deal with the hurt and abused little girl I had hidden deep inside of me. In fact, the drugs made me forget the bad things and made me feel happy for once in my life. I could actually conquer my fears and forget my pain while I was high. The people I hung with accepted me and liked having me with them.

However, my grades started going down and I was becoming more and more rebellious. No matter what I did it seemed like the men around me were trying to take from me. One day, I was in a neighborhood house with a bunch of older men and girls. We had been drinking, smoking pot, and fooling around when we heard the cops pull up out front. I ran out the back door to find my mother waiting there for me. My mother had called the police and wanted them to arrest me. When they refused, she sent me to a girl's home for troubled teens. When I got out, my mother said she didn't want me at home alone and sent me to my sister's house. I think I was fourteen at the time.

Of course, I did not want to be there around my brother-in-law, but I was afraid to tell anyone what had happened with him. On my fifteenth birthday, he got my sister and me drunk. My sister passed out first and then I finally passed out, too. The next morning, I woke to my brother-in-law raping me, but this time my sister walked in on us. She blamed me, though he did tell her he imitated it. He neglected to tell her about all the previous times, however. She threw me out. I was fifteen at the time.

Marriage and a Family

I had been dating a neighbor since I was thirteen and when I told him and his parents I had no place to go, they took me in. They treated me like their own daughter and finally their son and I decided to get married. I was sixteen when we married. He was a great guy and I started working as a waitress to help support us. Our marriage was wonderful and things were going great. We had a son together when I was eighteen. When I went back to work after my baby was born, I was working as a waitress, but not making much money. My husband met some guys who told him how much money we could make if I began working at the strip club. We decided I would take the job. I would work nights and he would be home with our son.

I actually liked all the attention and it made me feel really pretty. I was making a lot of money in tips, too. Some nights I would have $100 bills tucked into what little clothing I was wearing. One particular client that really seemed to like my dancing, began giving me $100 bills with white powder rolled up in them. When I got back into the dressing room with the other strippers, I would dump the white powder in the garbage can. One of them saw me doing it and told me not to waste it and to put it in the "happy powder" can.

After that, I was more observant of these girls. They would snort that powder and then danced very exotically. The clients really seemed to like this so one night I decided to try it, too. For the next six months, I danced and used cocaine. By the time my son was one-year old, I was addicted to crack cocaine. I took my son, left my first husband, and ran off with my drug dealer who had been wining and dining me. He had been treating me like a princess. However, it didn't take him long to realize he did not want me and my little son in his life.

Rejected again, feeling used and abused, I began to rely more and more on my first husband's parents to help raise and care for my son. They were actually wonderful. If they saw me on the street, instead of condemning me and turning their backs on me like my own family had, they would invite me in, let me shower, see my son, and feed me.

> *Do not judge and criticize and condemn others, so that you may not be judged and criticized and condemned yourselves. For just as you judge and criticize and condemn others, you will be judged and criticized and condemned, and in accordance with the measure you [use to] deal out to others, it will be dealt out again to you.* (Matthew 7:1-2 AMP)

However, I had the presence of mind to realize how badly I was addicted to drugs and did not think it was safe for my son to live with me, so I gave his aunt custody of him. In my mind, I would get cleaned up and then eventually come back for him. However, I had a very long hard road ahead of me before I would ever get the chance to be a mother and have a family again. Even after I divorced my husband, his parents were still caring and concerned about me.

Out On My Own

Now, with no husband and no child to care for, living with my new guy started out fine. He was giving me so much attention and we seemed to always have enough drugs and could pretty much stay high most of the time as long as I continued stripping. Then one night the guy I was living with was arrested and taken to jail. When I ran out of drugs, I went looking for the dope house where I knew he had been buying the drugs. The problem was I did not know the guy I was living with owed these big time dealers a lot of money. When they found out he had gone to jail, they decided they were going to come after me to pay his bills.

When I showed up at the drug house, these guys were not there, but one of the guys that knew me, liked me, and warned me they were after me. Before I could get out of there, he saw them coming up the front sidewalk. He hid me in his room and told them I had been there but had left. Then he told me I could stay a few nights until I could figure out what I was going to do.

Three nights later, these guys showed up unannounced and walked in on me in his room before I could hide. They told me I owed the drug dealer's debt and they were going to collect it one way or the other. To prove how serious they were, they heated up a crack pipe and began to burn me all over my body. I don't remember if they left me for dead or how I escaped, but I know God must have been watching over me. I believe they intended to kill me. However, the next thing I knew I was running for my life fearing they were chasing me.

I ran for hours through the mud and dirt trying to stay out of sight. I had a friend in a nearby city and showed up there all dirty, burned, and bleeding. She took me in, helped me clean up, and I stayed with her for a while. Afraid to go back to the old area, I went back to work as a stripper in the area where my friend lived. I told her as soon as I made enough money I would find a place of my own. That is when I met the most beautiful black woman I had ever met. She invited me to stay with her and introduced me to a whole new way to make money – prostitution.

From the Street to the Cross

Do not judge and criticize and condemn others, so that you
may not be judged and criticized and condemned yourselves.
For just as you judge and criticize and condemn others, you
will be judged and criticized and condemned, and in accor-
dance with the measure you [use to] deal out to others, it will
be dealt out again to you. (Matthew 7:1-2 AMP)

Many times we look at people living on the street, whether they are homeless or prostitutes, and we are tempted to judge them for the choices they are making. We often think they just need to stop and get their lives straightened out. We need to ask God to reveal His heart for all of His children and seek ways to help these people instead of condemning them.

Matthew 7:1-2 warns us not to _____ because
_____.
Is this something you need to work on in your own life? _____

Ask Yourself...

Have I made some poor choices in my life?
What affect have these choices made on my journey
through life?

How would you counsel others to avoid making these kinds of choices? _____
How would you help someone you know who is heading on such a destructive path?_____

Pray and ask God to fill your heart with compassion instead of criticism. Ask Him to begin to show you how you might help others not make the same mistakes you have made.

Chapter 2

Out of the Frying Pan and into the Fire

My new friend really seemed to care about me and said she had found a way to survive on the streets. She said she could train me and help me earn the money I would need to not only survive but thrive. I liked the sound of this since I was on my own, afraid to go back to my old stomping ground, and didn't even have a high school education. She told me I could earn money and be paid for what other men had been taking from me. This beautiful woman seemed to have a great life so I told her I wanted in.

I entered the world of prostitution at the age of twenty-one and spent the next several years on the streets as a working girl. The lady that introduced me to this life began to teach me the tricks of the trade. Next thing I knew, I was out doing tricks. Life on the streets was exciting and scary all at the same time. I met a lot of weirdos who asked me to do strange things, but the girls I worked with became my family. We had each other's backs. My past did not matter to these girls because they all had a story to tell, too. Many had been abused like me and never felt they could tell anyone about it. We could tell each other anything and were never judged or condemned or rejected by one another.

We would hang together on the street for protection. One of us always knew where the others were. Sometimes we would approach a vehicle together and sort of check out the occupant before one of us would get in. Then when the night was over, we would seek a place to stay together to sleep and rest. We often stayed in abandoned houses without running water and no electric, but we had a roof over our heads and felt we were protected from the elements and the dangers of the street life while we slept.

Once in a while we would find a benefactor who let us either stay in one of his vacant houses or would charge us a minimal rent. We did stay in a motel almost one whole year, pooling our money to pay the rent. The owner knew what we were doing, but as long as we agreed not to bring anyone to the room, paid our weekly rent, and did not cause any drama he was cool with it.

I really enjoyed staying at this motel. There was a donut shop right in front of it and I learned that every night at 2:00 a.m. they would put all the leftover donuts into a big trash bag and toss it into the dumpster behind the shop. I would run up and grab the bag and take it to our room. Then we would eat donuts to our heart's content!

One time I did have a client drop me off too close to the motel. Though I took a roundabout route back, he was able to follow me close enough to figure out I was staying someplace in the motel and staked out the place. Once he figured it out, he showed up at my door and was trying to strangle me because I wouldn't go with him when my drug dealer showed up and ran him off. Later he came back and put a box outside the door then he called in a bomb threat to the motel manager. The manager called the bomb squad, they caught the guy, and the owner moved me to a different section of the motel after that which was pretty decent of him considering all the drama it caused. However, I lost the room when I got arrested and wasn't there to pay the rent.

Seven Years on the Street

I learned a lot living and working on the street. The first two years, I was very naïve and did pretty much whatever the client wanted me to do. As I grew and gained more confidence, I learned from the other girls what not to do. Sometimes I learned the hard way, like never take a client to where you live. I brought one guy back to where we were living and we partied and got high. He went after me with a crowbar when I told him he had to leave. Then he came back later looking for me and threatened my friends when they wouldn't tell him where I was. However, most of the time my work was done in their car or truck. Though I sometimes wondered about a client, most of the time I was pretty fearless, almost feeling I was invincible.

I also learned that drug dealers would say they liked you and wanted to take care of you, but they were not faithful or loyal. Drug dealers lived in a very dangerous world which often spilled over into whoever was around them.

Once in a while I would meet someone who really seemed to care about me and truly wanted to help me get off the streets, off drugs, and out of the business.

Andy was one of those guys. He would let me rent from him and wanted me to at least get off drugs. Sometimes he would go to extremes to try and get me to clean up my act. One time he saw me on the street and told me I looked tired and sick and needed to come back with him and get some rest. This time he was really concerned that I was so drugged up and had not eaten or slept that I would send myself to an early grave. He took

25

me to home, locked me in, bolted all the windows and doors and took out all of the tools I could use to try and escape. He told me to sleep it off and he would be back with some new clothes and food for me in a little while.

I probably would have slept there and taken him up on his offer to help me if he had not locked me in. The locked windows and doors presented a challenge I could not resist. I tore the place apart and found a butter knife that I used to take the front door off its hinges. I left the door in the side yard and took off.

Then there was Old Man Casey who was a harmless old pervert. He would let us hang out at his house, take showers, play cards, and relax. All he wanted in exchange was pictures of us. It was nice to have a safe house to go to where very little was expected of us in return.

Close Encounters of the Dangerous Kind

During those years on the street, I had many close calls. When I look back I see how God was there watching over me the whole time, though I admit it took me many years to come to that conclusion.

One night I was walking the streets very late at night. I should have gone in by then, but agreed to take one more job. I got into the guy's truck and he took off at high speed. When he stopped in an unlit deserted area, he beat me up, raped me, and left me out in the middle of nowhere when he was done with me. It took me hours to find my way back to our place.

I have had knives and razor blades held against my throat, and guns pointed at my head. One guy told me he was going to kill me shortly after I got into his truck, so I reached for the door handle determined to jump out even though he was going at a pretty high speed. I got the door handle and opened it trying to jump out. He grabbed for my blouse and dragged me along the side of the truck until the shirt ripped off of me. Though I was covered in road rash, I was still alive. As soon as I was free of the truck, I was up and running like my life depended on it. Somehow, he couldn't find me or gave up looking and I escaped again through the grace of God.

One year there was a family of psychos who posed as drug dealers, but were out to kill prostitutes. Two of the girls I hung out with became their victims. One of them was found wrapped in a carpet after they had killed her and the other had been beaten with a pipe and then set on fire. They determined later that the Tasmanian Killers were enraged because one of them had contracted HIV from a prostitute. They were on some kind of personal vendetta.

Many times we would have regular clients which we liked because once we knew them we felt safe with them. However, one of my regular guys came for me one night and said he wanted to do drugs with me as well this time. He took me back to his house. I should have known something wasn't right when he locked the doors as soon as we got into the house.

This guy had always seemed like a nice guy, but when he started doing drugs, he became a monster. He would take a hit and then do something to me to hurt me. He would beat me or rape me or try to strangle me after each hit. Finally, I told him we were out of dope and we needed to go get some more. He told me he would go get it, but I convinced him they would never sell to him because they did not know him. I told him they would only sell to me.

We got into his car and he held a knife to my side the whole way to the dope house. I convinced him he couldn't come to the door with me, but he could see me from the car and I wouldn't go in anyway. I knew the drug dealer, though, and when I told him the guy had been threatening me, he let me in and I ran out the back door before the guy in the car figured out what was going on. When the guy went to the door asking for me, the drug dealer threatened him if he didn't get out of there.

Another regular client of mine was this big black guy who always wore a big cross around his neck. He was always nice to me until one night he took me to the end of a deserted road. We only passed one house and there were no street lights or anything around. He pulled out a gun, told me to take all of my clothes off, he raped me, and then said he was going to kill me. Somehow, I got out of the car and ran naked to the house we had passed. There were no lights on and I wasn't even sure if there was anyone living in it. I got into the garage and hid behind a washer and dryer.

An old man turned on the lights and came out into the garage having heard me moving around out there. I told him what was going on and he wrapped me in a blanket, gave me some clothes, and drove me back to the main street. I never saw the black man with the cross again. Later, I heard he was murdered. I thank God the old man in the house was there when I needed him and was willing to help me.

One of the things the girls eventually taught me to do was "stiff" the clients. We especially liked to stiff married men. We felt they shouldn't be with us and that they should be home with their wives. We would demand the money up front and then run off with it without providing any service. Sometimes we would work together as a team. One of us would connect with the client, take them to a rented motel room that we had predetermined. One of us would be under the bed and the other would be his girl. Though he did get what he paid for, the other girl would clean out his wallet while he was otherwise occupied. It was a dangerous game as we were about to discover.

One time we stiffed a father of one of the large gangs in the area without realizing it. We were smart enough to never keep the wallet or steal credit cards so they couldn't prove it was us that stole from them, but they were out to get us anyways. Knowing the police wouldn't do anything about it, they came after us themselves. They found out where we were working, but we saw them coming and ran out of there as fast as we could and hid under a neighbor's front porch. We could see them searching for us, but they couldn't do too much out in the open like that, so they eventually left us alone. Once again, God had my back.

Human Trafficking

In 1993, I was sitting in a crack house when a guy came to buy dope and sat down next to me. After we had talked for a while, he invited me to his house for a more intimate party. He was the perfect gentleman until we got inside his house. Then he dead bolted the door and grabbed me by the neck. He started to strangle me, then raped me, and continued slapping me across the face. When he seemed to be finished with me, in walked his wife. To my surprise she didn't seemed at all surprised and told me to get up and come with her to take a shower. She took what was left of my clothes and then took me to a bedroom where I was given very minimal attire. The windows were covered and barred. Looking around I knew I was in trouble.

The following day they opened the bedroom door and let one of their friends in to visit with me. I was told to do whatever their friend wanted me to do. Then I was fed and told to rest until they had need of me again. I was kept there for three weeks. They even gave me a little dope so I wouldn't be in such bad shape I couldn't service their clients. Once or twice I was taken to another house, locked in a bedroom, and sent clients to service them. Then they would come back and get me and return me to their house. I now know what they were doing was human trafficking.

Apparently one time they were asked by a wealthy client to bring me to the client's house. He did not want to be seen entering the human trafficker's house. They loaded me up in a car. My "owner" was in the back seat and the two drug dealers were in the front with a gun on us all the time. There appeared to be disagreement between the man in the front seat and my "owner." It sounded like my "owner" owed these guys some money and I was to help defer the debt by servicing this wealthy client.

However, when we arrived at the client's house, there was no one there. It was already dark so they argued about whether or not to wait. My "owner" told the guys to make sure their guns were out of sight. He suggested we slowly drive around the block and wait for the client to come and then he could pay his debt.

All of a sudden, two things happened that could have only been orchestrated by God. As they argued in the front seat, none of the men were paying any attention to me. I saw headlights coming at us, and I heard a voice in my head say, "Jump!"

The car I was in was moving slowly, so I opened the door and jumped out right in front of the oncoming headlights. The car coming at me screeched to a halt and I took off running. I was afraid the other guys were going to chase me, so I ran without looking back. I'm not sure exactly what happened, but I found out later that the human trafficker was arrested that night and I never saw or heard from any of them again.

Looking back, I think it was God who told me to jump right at that moment. He had plans for me and He was going to make sure I had every opportunity to fulfill them in spite of my poor decisions along the way.

> *For I know the plans I have for you," declares the LORD,*
> *"plans to prosper you and not to harm you, plans to give you*
> *hope and a future.* (Jeremiah 29:11 NIV)

From the Street to the Cross

I had many close encounters, but when I look back I see how God was there watching over me the whole time, though it took me many years to come to that conclusion. I am so thankful God had a plan for me and was determined I would live to fulfill it. He is definitely a God of second chances. I am living proof of His love and His grace.

What does Jeremiah 29:11 say about God's plan for you?

_____

His plans are to give you _____ and _____.

Ask Yourself...

Have I ever had a time when looking back I should not have made it out of a bad situation, but somehow I did?

Can I now see how God had His hand on me and was helping me get to where He could fulfill His purpose in my life?

Pray and ask God to reveal His plan and purpose for your life as you spend time praying and reading His word, the Bible. Thank Him for the times He has rescued you from your poor decisions. Ask Him for wisdom as you go through this day.

Chapter 3

God's Ways Are Higher than Ours

"For My thoughts are not your thoughts, nor are your ways My ways," says the LORD. (Isaiah 55:8 NKJV)

So many times God proved to me that He was in control, though it took me many years to really understand that His ways are so much higher than ours. I kept looking for a way out and all He wanted me to do was to start turning to Him. Later in life I read the parable Jesus told about the prodigal son and one phrase really stood out for me.

When he came to his senses... (Luke 15:17 NIV)

Jail / Rehab Time

In spite of my drug habit, I saved enough money to buy a little car. I was so proud of my car. In all my years on the street, I had never really owned anything. I loved my little car. Then one night I was involved in a hit and run accident. Even though I was not at fault, I was under the influence so I took off and left the scene. They even had a police helicopter following me. Not thinking it through, I made my way to Old Man Casey's and they found me there and arrested me. I spent a year in jail that time. Prior to this time in jail, I had been arrested probably nine times.

Jail time always ended up being a sort of a blessing in disguise for me. It actually turned into rehab time for me. I would not do any drugs, I would meet people who taught me about God, and I always vowed I would never go back to life on the streets once I got out. In spite of all my good intentions, when I was released back out into the world, my world had not really changed and I inevitably ended up back with the same crowd doing the same things.

One time I spent time in jail for something I really didn't do. I had been living with a guy and we partied a lot. We really enjoyed doing crack together. One day we ran out of drugs and neither of us had any money. I told him I could sell his speakers and then I could get some more drugs and I would be able to stay with him a while longer. He liked me and wanted me to stay so he took me where I told him to and we sold the speakers. We did the drugs and when they ran out, I once again suggested we sell something else of his to get some more. Well, I guess he didn't like me that much because unbeknownst to me, he called the cops and told them I had stolen his speakers. I was charged with grand theft and did a year in jail for a crime I did not commit.

Once I was arrested for possession, and the cops told me they would be lenient if I would help them bring down some of the drug dealers. They were after bigger fish than me. I knew better than to go against the drug dealers so I said I wouldn't do it. However, they told me they would give me some money to go buy the drugs, give me a ride to the drug house, and then let me keep some of the drugs after the bust. This time I agreed, but on the way there I decided I could make the best of both worlds and not be labeled a rat by the drug dealers. I went to the door of the drug house, told the drug dealer that the cops had sent me and were waiting to arrest him. He invited me in, we went out through the back garage and he took me with him. He gave me some drugs for letting him know the cops were on to him. A month later, the cops found me and I did a year in jail charging me with prostitution for not snitching.

I did serious jail time a total of fourteen times during my years on the street and was arrested probably seventeen or eighteen other times. Three times I served a full one-year sentence for major crimes. God sent so many great people across my path during those times in jail. Each one planted seeds that would later help lead me to where God wanted me to be.

One of the times I was in jail, I met a young girl who had contracted HIV as a prostitute. She read her Bible and prayed and asked God to help her. She took her meds and stood on her new found faith. Later, when they tested her again, the results were negative. God had answered her sincere prayer and healed her. This made a lasting impression on me. I started going to church in jail and seeking Him. The song "Amazing Grace" is what kept me going many times after I got out.

I always believed there was a God, but I did not know what it was like to have a personal relationship with Jesus. Though I felt I was invincible, I was beginning to think there was something out there protecting me. It had happened too many times to be ignored. I kept reading the Bible, praying, and asking God to show me how to stop the drugs and get my life cleaned up. He answered my prayers in a series of divine appointments.

Amazing grace! How sweet the sound
That saved a wretch like me.
I once was lost, but now am found,

Was blind but now I see.[1]

Divine Appointments

There were so many times when I made a poor choice and put myself in harm's way. The dangerous practice of "stiffing" guys got me in trouble more times than I can count. One such time I had escaped from some armed gunmen by running out the back of the house we were in, but I was afraid they were still after me. I came around the corner of the grocery store on the corner and I saw the guys looking for me riding in the back of an open pick-up truck. Across the street near the motel were a group of about seven young black men. Thinking I only had a moment to get to them undetected by the guys in the pick-up truck, I made a dash for the black guys and slide around behind them asking them for help as some bad guys were after me.

One of the young men put me in the back seat of the car and told me to stay down on the floor. Then they all casually stood around the car so that no one could easily look inside. When the men in the pick-up truck asked if they had seen me they said a girl had just run around the corner in the other direction. After the gunmen left, the young black men offered to give me a ride to some place safe. When I asked them why they were helping me, they said they all had moms and sisters and would have wanted someone to help them if they were in trouble. Sure enough, they delivered me safely to where I was living at the time. Thank you, God for this divine appointment. I know He had those young men waiting there to protect me that night.

---

[1] "Amazing Grace How Sweet the Sound," *Dictionary of American Hymnology*. Retrieved on October 31, 2009. Written by English poet and clergyman John Newton.

Then I met this seventy-year-old black lady one day as I was out walking the street near her house. She walked right up to me and said, "Come here little lady. You look tired. Come with me and let me clean you up." Once I got to her house, she told me to take a shower, then sent me to go to bed to get some sleep. When I woke up, she had a brand new outfit ready for me to put on. Then she invited me into her kitchen and taught me how to cook the most amazing meals. She was so patient and kind.

Every time she saw me it was the same routine. She told me once when we were cooking together, "To be a good chef you must cook with love. When you do, the entire meal will be scrumptious!" She not only cooked with love, her life demonstrated God's love. She looked passed my current condition and saw me as I could be if someone would take the time to invest in me. She inspired me to do the same for others once I did get my life straightened out.

Then there was Toby, who really tried to help me get off the street and off drugs. He worked at building HUD houses and took me with him as he traveled to NY, NJ, and other places around the states. I really liked him and thought I had found a way to get off the streets for good. Then I found out he had other girls he was keeping in several other locations doing the same thing. I was jealous and felt he was cheating on me so I left him.

Having tasted the possibility of life off the streets, I went back to the life, but I kept looking for my way out. I met Brad, who was a drug dealer, but he really seemed to like me and care about me. I thought I had finally found a place to stay and a man to stay with. I lived with him for nine months and then I discovered he was cheating on me with other prostitutes of all things.

I left him, hurt and disappointed. I hit rock bottom feeling that he had been my last chance at happiness. Though he was not my knight in shining armor, he was part of God's plan for me. In fact, soon after I moved in with Brad, I prayed I would get pregnant so he would want me to stay and we could become a family. I promised God if I could have another child that I could keep and raise, I would never do drugs or prostitute myself ever again.

Thinking God and Brad had both let me down, I went back out on the street. It just so happened I was back on the street the very day the health department was doing their health-check round up. Every so often they would pull us all in for blood tests and checkups. They were trying to prevent the spread of the HIV virus so that was their main purpose for bringing us all in. During the course of my exam, they discovered I was pregnant. Shocked and then elated, I immediately sought out my parole officer. I knew God had answered my prayer though not exactly as I had thought He would.

Now I needed a way off the street. I told my parole officer I wanted off the street for good. I told him I was pregnant and asked him to "violate me" which meant he would cite me for a parole violation so I would be arrested. I knew if I was in jail I would not be tempted to go back to drugs and I would have medical help all through my pregnancy. What I wanted was to be able to be protected during my pregnancy, have my baby, and then leave jail to raise the child. I thought it was a great plan, but my parole officer said the system didn't work that way.

Apparently, I really had to seriously break the law in order to get him to have me arrested. Desperate now, I decided to take things into my own hands. I bought an army knife and robbed someone of $3,000 at knife point. Sure enough I was arrested. I spent a month in jail awaiting trial. When I appeared before the judge with a public defender representing me, he said he was going to sentence me to five years in prison.

When I realized that a five-year prison sentence would prevent me from keeping my baby, I jumped up out of my seat. Even though the public defender advised me to sit down and be quiet, I asked the judge for permission to speak. He allowed me to plead my case.

"Your Honor, I have been in out of jail ten times. I have never been sent to a rehab to help me change my life so when I got out I could truly start over instead of going back to the same destructive life style. Now I am pregnant and I want to go to rehab, get my life in order, and then have a real chance to raise my child. Please, Your Honor," I pleaded. "Send me to a rehab! I promise that if you do, you will never see me stand in front of you again!"

I think both the judge and God could see that I had come to my senses. Through the grace of God, he sentenced me to six months at the Salvation Army Rehab and a mandatory two-year house arrest. I knew God had moved on my behalf! He had answered my prayers above and beyond what I could have ever thought possible!

> *Now to Him Who, by (in consequence of) the [action of His] power that is at work within us, is able to [carry out His purpose and] do superabundantly, far over and above all that we [dare] ask or think [infinitely beyond our highest prayers, desires, thoughts, hopes, or dreams]—To Him be glory in the church and in Christ Jesus throughout all generations forever and ever. Amen (so be it).* (Ephesians 3:20-21 AMP)

I did indeed begin to attend meetings for the next year and met a woman who became my best friend. When my second son was born, the Salvation Army provided a home for me to live in with my son. I refused to go backwards. I kept my focus on God and was determined to move forward. God honored His promise and I honored mine. Now I just wanted to serve this God who had so amazingly provided for me and my son!

From the Street to the Cross

When I finally came to my senses, God was able to help me help myself. In the story of the prodigal son, I love the part where it says while his son was still a long way off, the father saw him, ran to him, threw his arms around his son, and kissed him. It is so obvious this father had been watching for his son's return and welcomed him back with open arms.

That is how I see Father God. He was watching me, protecting me, and waiting for me to come to my senses and run into His waiting arms. When I did, then He could give me all the blessings He had planned for me and they were above and beyond what I could have ever imagined.

Read Luke 15:11-24.

Did the father in the parable condemn his son for squandering his wealth in wild living? _____ How do you know that? _____

_____

What finally caused the son to come to his senses?

_____

The boy offered to become one of the father's servants, but what did the father do?

_____

_____

Why did the father do all of this? _____

If God would do this for someone like me, He will surely do it for you as well if you will just turn and run into His waiting arms.

Ask Yourself...

> *Do I now see my heavenly Father like the father in the parable Jesus told?*
> *Have I been like the lost son?*
> *Will I come to my senses today and turn around and run into God's waiting arms?*

If this is your desire, get down on your knees and pray. Ask your loving Heavenly Father to forgive you for your sins. Then thank Him for loving and forgiving you. Next ask Him to help you begin to change your life. Ask Him what He wants you to change. One of the ways to begin to learn His ways is to begin to read the Bible.

The best way is to begin in the second half of the Bible and start reading the Book of John. This book will tell you about the life of Jesus and why God loves you no matter what condition you are in. Then read Matthew, Mark, and Luke. These will give you more information about the life of Jesus. I have offered a study plan for you at the end of this book to help you get started.

Find a Bible teaching church and a study partner—someone who can answer your questions as you read and study God's written word. Remember, if you are confused all you have to do is pray. God is there for you every minute of every day. I have also given you my contact information at the end of the book so you can connect with me. I am here to help you. God sent others to help me so I will be there for you as well.

Chapter 4

Living in the Palm of His Hand

*But God is faithful [to His Word and to His compassionate nature], and He [can be trusted] not to let you be tempted and tried and assayed beyond your ability and strength of resistance and power to endure, but with the temptation He will [always] also provide the way out (**the means of escape to a landing place**), that you may be capable and strong and powerful to bear up under it patiently.* (1 Corinthians 10:13 AMP emphasis added)

God is so amazing! Not only was I cared for and given a home for my son and I, they helped me find a job. I began to work at Taco Bell. I never thought I could do anything but live on the streets, but now I was supporting my child, living a life I was not ashamed of, and where both of us were safe. God had provided a way of escape from that destructive life and given me a safe and nurturing environment to live in and raise my son.

However, as I continued to grow and thrive, God showed me He had even more in store for me. While I was working at Taco Bell, I met a man who ran a commercial cleaning company. He hired me to work for him.

We would go into these big office buildings and clean after the business was closed. I worked my way up in his company to supervisor and began to feel really good about myself. God was beginning to reveal to me how He saw me, not how the world had labeled me.

As my self-esteem began to improve, I began to date. I met and married again. He and I and my son had a beautiful life together and I gave birth to a beautiful daughter. I really thought this was the man I would be married to the rest of my life. Then I discovered he was cheating on me. This was something I could not tolerate, so I divorced him.

Unfortunately, I still had not learned to go to God when it came to my relationships with men. A year later I married again. I thought this was the man God had brought into my life, but he was not only a counterfeit, this man was sent by the enemy to distract me and try to ruin my life. The enemy did not like that I was beginning to tell my story and encourage girls who were living and working on the streets to turn to God.

I started clubbing and drinking. Then this man began to abuse me verbally and physically. He told me I was no good, would never amount to anything, and that I was lucky to have him because no other man would ever want me. Not only did he break both my knees, and beat and choke me, he tried to break my spirit as well. He threatened to come after me and kill me if I ever left him. However, God provided a way of escape from this abusive relationship and kept my children safe as well.

> *Jesus said, "The thief comes only in order to steal and kill and destroy. I came that they may have and enjoy life, and have it in abundance (to the full, till it overflows)." (John 10:10 AMP)*

Jesus also told His disciples, "In the world you have tribulation and trials and distress and frustration; but be of good cheer [take courage; be confident, certain, undaunted]! For I have overcome the world. [I have deprived it of power to harm you and have conquered it for you.]" (John 16:33 AMP).

I was baptized on January 28, 2015 which was the day my divorce was final from this man who I should never have married. That was also the day my life changed dramatically knowing God was in control and I could truly count on Him to fulfill all of my needs. I stopped clubbing, drinking, and smoking and started going to church every Sunday.

We can stand on these promises and my life proves it. God began to remind me who He said I was and showed me how He saw me. He said He would be my husband and provide for me and my children. When I turned this area of my life over to God, He once again led me out of a bad situation and helped me get back on the path He had chosen for me. God is all about our success in life. He is 100 percent for us and wants to see us prosper so we can bring hope to others. Though we will all face difficulties in life, God is always there for us if we will just remember to go to Him first.

> *But seek (aim at and strive after) first of all His kingdom and His righteousness (His way of doing and being right), and then all these things taken together will be given you besides.* (Matthew 6:33 AMP)

As I worked my way up within the cleaning company, I saw times when my employer would turn down cleaning jobs that he considered too small. Since he didn't want the business, I started doing these smaller jobs on the side and starting my own business. Eventually, I was able to quit working for the other company and now my company has grown from just a few accounts to seventeen commercial buildings and seven employees. Doing things God's way has caused me to prosper, and I want to let my light shine so others will see how much He loves us and wants to bless us with all that He has for us. He has called me to be a motivational speaker and tell my story as a way to give hope and light to a darkened world.

> ***You are the light of the world.*** *A city set on a hill cannot be hidden. Nor do men light a lamp and put it under a peck measure, but on a lampstand, and it gives light to all in the house. Let your light so shine before men that they may see your moral excellence and your praiseworthy, noble, and good deeds and recognize and honor and praise and glorify your Father Who is in heaven.* (Matthew 5:14-16 AMP)

> *Let the message of Christ dwell among you richly as you teach and admonish one another with all wisdom through psalms, hymns, and songs from the Spirit, singing to God with gratitude in your hearts.* (Colossians 3:16 NIV)

From the Street to the Cross

I lived on the street for many years, but I never caught Aids and I survived many near death experiences because God not only loved me, He wanted me to move forward and fulfill what I was born and designed to do. In order to bring me from the street to the cross, He had to show me how much He loved me and who He said I was. When I met Jesus Christ and learned what He and God the Father had done for me, I began to see His Amazing Grace. It was believing His truth and not the world's lies that has truly set me free and given me the strength to rise above my past and move into my God ordained future.

> *"And you will know the truth, and the truth will set you free."* (John 8:32 NLT)

Read these scriptures, learn the truth of who God says you are, and use them to describe yourself. Never believe the lies of the enemy and the world ever again.

John 16:27 says I am _____

John 15:16 says I have been _____

Matthew 5:13-14 says God has chosen me to

_____

1 Peter 2:4 says I am _____ to God.

2 Corinthians 5:20 says He has called me to be His

_____

Romans 8:16 says I am a child of _____

Thank your heavenly Father for His love and for accepting you as His beloved child.

> *But seek (aim at and strive after) first of all His kingdom and His righteousness (His way of doing and being right), and then all these things taken together will be given you besides.* (Matthew 6:33 AMP)

Ask Yourself...

> *Am I seeking to do things God's way?*

Am I a light shining out God's love to others?
What is God asking me to do so that others can see how much He loves them?

Ask God to show you what it is He is calling you to do with your life so that you can truly be His light to a darkened world.

Conclusion

The Devil Is a Liar, God Is Truth

*He [the devil] was a murderer from the beginning and does not stand in the truth, because there is no truth in him. When he speaks a falsehood, he speaks what is natural to him, **for he is a liar** [himself] and the father of lies and of all that is false.* (John 8:44 AMP emphasis)

*God is not a human being, and **he will not lie**. He is not a human, and he does not change his mind. What he says he will do, he does. **What he promises, he makes come true.*** (Numbers 23:19 NCV emphasis added)

Today, I am still an outcast in my family. My sister is still married to the man who abused me as a child and still blames me for the incident she witnessed that day. I know I made many bad choices along the way, but even after all these years, my mom still says everything that has happened to me is my own fault.

When I reached out to my biological father asking him to help me and my two kids get away from my second husband and that abusive relationship, he told me to never call again and that he wasn't my dad. I haven't heard from him or seen him since.

For many years I believed the lies the devil sent my way. He even used my family to deceive me into thinking I was no good and would never amount to anything. The enemy used some of the people I encountered along my life journey to reinforce his lies and he tried to take me out more than once.

However, I want to tell the world how good God is. In spite of those choices, God has not condemned nor rejected me. He has never lied to me. What He says He will do, He does it, and He always keeps His promises! He has even helped me to learn to forgive those who abused me.

There is a story in the Bible about a woman who was caught in the act of adultery. She was sleeping with a married man. The local religious leaders wanted to condemn her. Their laws said she deserved to die. There are many people even in today's world that would condemn the girls who live and work on the streets. These people have no idea what drove these girls to choose that lifestyle. They look at these working girls, homeless people, and drug addicts with distain and say they deserve what they get. Many people think they should just be arrested and locked away from society. Is that really what God says?

These religious leaders of the day brought this woman who was caught in adultery to Jesus. They reminded Jesus that the law said she should be condemned and stoned to death. I find it interesting that the law also said the man she was with was guilty of adultery against his wife and should have also been condemned and stoned. In fact, in Matthew 5:28 Jesus said, "But I say to you that whoever looks at a woman to lust for her has already committed adultery with her in his heart" (NKJV). However, these religious leaders did not bring the man before Jesus, only the woman.

As I read this story, I felt Jesus was talking to me and that He was not condemning me either.

> *Then the scribes and Pharisees brought to Him a woman caught in adultery. And when they had set her in the midst, they said to Him, "Teacher, this woman was caught in adultery, in the very act. Now Moses, in the law, commanded us that such should be stoned. But what do You say?" So when they continued asking Him, He raised Himself up and said to them, "He who is without sin among you, let him throw a stone at her first." Then those who heard it, being convicted by their conscience, went out one by one, beginning with the oldest even to the last. And Jesus was left alone, and the woman standing in the midst. When Jesus had raised Himself up and saw no one but the woman, He said to her, "Woman, where are those accusers of yours? Has no one condemned you?" She said, "No one, Lord." And Jesus said to her, "**Neither do I condemn you; go and sin no more.**"*
> (John 8:3-5, 7, 9-11 NKJV emphasis added)

Not only did I feel Jesus was not condemning me, He also showed in Mark 9:42 that those who bully, betray the trust of, and hurt innocent boys and girls causing them to sin are the ones that should be punished. Jesus said, "On the other hand, if you give one of these simple, childlike believers a hard time, bullying or taking advantage of their simple trust, you'll soon wish you hadn't. You'd be better off dropped in the middle of the lake with a millstone around your neck" (MSG). Many of the girls I lived with on the street had been abused as children. Most of them had been too afraid to tell anyone or if they did, they were not believed. These children felt they were the problem and grew up to a life full of guilt and shame. They need to hear the words of Jesus like I did and that is what I hope to do.

Compassion Not Condemnation

There is a story about another woman that was an outcast of her family and looked down upon by the whole town in which she lived. She lived in guilt and shame until she had an encounter with Jesus that changed her life forever. This woman came to well one day to draw water and was surprised to find a Rabbi sitting there. She came during the heat of the day to avoid meeting up with anyone from her village. She knew what they all thought of her. However, before she could turn around and leave, Jesus spoke to her and asked her to get Him a cup of water from the well (John 4:4-9).

She was totally shocked! First of all, Jesus was a Jew and Jews never interact with Samaritans, especially not a Samaritan woman. Thinking this Rabbi did not know who she was, she pointed out His error and even boldly challenged Him for how the Jews treated Samaritans. Jesus then said some amazing things to her.

In John 4:10 Jesus said to her, "If you knew the gift of God and who it is that asks you for a drink, you would have asked him and he would have given you living water" (NIV).

She, of course, asked Jesus to give her this living water thinking it would save her from having to go to the well every day. At that point, Jesus revealed He knew all about her. He told her to go and get her husband and then He would talk with both of them about this living water. Though she figured telling Him the truth would end the conversation, she told Him she did not have a husband.

Then Jesus shocked her by saying, "You are right when you say you have no husband. The fact is, you have had five husbands, and the man you now have is not your husband. What you have just said is quite true" (John 4:17-18 NIV).

There it was. Jesus knew she was living in sin, that she had been a woman of the streets, and was now an outcast. When she looked into His eyes she probably expected to see condemnation, but instead she saw compassion. I imagine she had never seen anyone, especially a man, look at her the way Jesus did. Instead of running away and hiding, she further engaged Him and asked Him the questions that were burning in her soul. I believe she was not happy with the life she was living and was truly seeking a way out.

Then in John 4:23-26, Jesus told her the most amazing truths about God and even revealed to her who He really was, something He had not even revealed to His closest disciples!

> *"Yet a time is coming and has now come when the true worshipers will worship the Father in the Spirit and in truth, for they are the kind of worshipers the Father seeks. God is spirit, and his worshipers must worship in the Spirit and in truth."* *The woman said, "I know that Messiah (called Christ) is coming. When he comes, he will explain everything to us."* **Then Jesus declared, "I, the one speaking to you—I am he."** (NIV emphasis added)

These stories about how Jesus treated the outcasts have inspired me to not only get my own life straightened out, but to reach out and help the girls and boys that are scared to tell about how they have been inappropriately touched and abused against their will. Having lived the street life and been addicted to drugs, I also want to help people who think they are trapped in the cycle of drug abuse. The message I have for them is the devil is a liar and God is the truth.

After Jesus revealed the truth to the Samaritan woman at the well, she took what she had learned back to her village and **shouted** it to everyone, including the men who knew her and used her. She gave her testimony to all of those who considered her an outcast. She became a witness for Jesus. That has been my heart's desire as well.

> *Then, leaving her water jar, the woman went back to the town and said to the people, "Come, see a man who told me everything I ever did. Could this be the Messiah?" They came out of the town and made their way toward him.* ***Many of the Samaritans from that town believed in him because of the woman's testimony,*** *"He told me everything I ever did." So when the Samaritans came to him, they urged him to stay with them, and he stayed two days. And because of his words many more became believers.* (John 4:28-30, 39-41 NIV emphasis added)

This outcast woman, who had been married five times and was currently living in sin, got radically transformed by her encounter with Jesus and instantly became a witness to those who would have surely condemned her. Her testimony led many people from her town to Jesus. If Jesus could use her to bring others to Him, I believe He can use me as well. I trust Him, I believe what His word, the Bible says is true, and I desire to thank Him for all He has done for me by helping others.

These two things cannot change: God cannot lie when he makes a promise, and he cannot lie when he makes an oath. These things encourage us who came to God for safety. They give us strength to hold on to the hope we have been given. (Hebrews 6:18 NCV)

From the Street to the Cross

Trust in the Lord with all your heart and lean not on your own understanding; in all your ways submit to him, and he will make your paths straight. (Proverbs 3:5-6 NIV)

Finding someone to trust while living on the streets was difficult. My trust had been violated when I was still a child, so believing someone could be trusted was difficult for me. However, I found that I could totally trust God.

The Lord is my strength and my shield; my heart trusts in him, and he helps me. My heart leaps for joy, and with my song I praise him. (Psalm 28:7 NIV)

What does John 8:44 say about the devil? _____
What does Numbers 23:19 say about God?

_____

What does Hebrews 6:18 say about God?

_____

Ask Yourself…

Will I finally put my trust in God and stop believing the lies of the enemy?

Will I firmly declare the truth of God and stop speaking the lies of the world to myself?

Will I begin to stand on the promises of God knowing He will do what He says He will do in my life?

Take what you have learned from reading my story and begin to apply God's truth to your life starting today. Begin by going through the Bible study provided for you at the end of this book. If God did it for me, He will surely do for you as well!

The LORD is on my side;
I will not fear.
What can man do to me?
The LORD is for me among those who help me;
Therefore I shall see my desire on those who hate me.
It is better to trust in the LORD
Than to put confidence in man.
It is better to trust in the LORD
Than to put confidence in princes.

The LORD is my strength and song,
And He has become my salvation.
I will praise You,
For You have answered me,
And have become my salvation.

You are my God, and I will praise You;
You are my God, I will exalt You.

Oh, give thanks to the LORD, for He is good!
For His mercy endures forever.

(Psalm 118:6-9, 14, 21, 28-29 NKJV)

About the Author

Misty Kinzel lives in Florida and is the mother of three beautiful children. She is a motivational speaker going out on the streets to help the people there to learn about the love of God and to give them hope for the future.

To contact Misty Kinzel or to book her as your motivational speaker, email her at: mistykinzel@gmail.com

Appendix

From the Street to the Cross Bible Study

"And you will know the truth, and the truth will set you free." (John 8:32 NLT)

he only way to learn the truth is to study God's word and get to know Him on a personal basis. This Bible study will help you learn who God is and about His great love for you as one of His children.

Make sure you have an easy to read modern Bible translation like New Living, Amplified or New Century Version. Also have a notebook or journal where you can record your thoughts as you move through the study. Ideally, sit down with your Bible, your journal, and spend time with God before you start your day, but the most important thing is to spend quality time with God studying His words of truth on a daily basis. This study will get you started by giving you a month's worth of short lessons. Once you have established the habit of spending time with Him, begin to explore the Bible further on your own or purchase another 30-day Bible study to guide you.

Week One: Our Incredible God

*Therefore, since we have been made right in God's sight by faith, we have peace with God because of what Jesus Christ our Lord has done for us. Because of our faith, **Christ has brought us into this place of undeserved privilege** where we now stand, and we confidently and joyfully look forward to sharing God's glory. We can rejoice, too, when we run into problems and trials, for we know that they help us develop endurance. And endurance develops strength of character, and character strengthens our confident hope of salvation. And this hope will not lead to disappointment. **For we know how dearly God loves us, because he has given us the Holy Spirit to fill our hearts with his love.** When we were utterly helpless, Christ came at just the right time and died for us sinners. Now, most people would not be willing to die for an upright person, though someone might perhaps be willing to die for a person who is especially good. **But God showed his great love for us by sending Christ to die for us while we were still sinners.** (Romans 5:1-8 NLT emphasis added)*

As you read in my story, God was there with me every step of the way even though I was not yet aware of it. What an incredible heavenly Father we have. He is incredibly patient with us, He loves us unconditionally, He keeps all of His promises to us, and wants to deliver us from all that would seek to destroy us. God is 100 percent for our success in this life. He wants to pour out the blessings of heaven upon us. Take the time this week to get to know your incredible heavenly Father. If He did this for me, He will do it for you as well.

Day One: God's Incredible Patience

One of the most amazing scriptures in the Bible is 2 Peter 3:9. Read it here in the Amplified Translation, but also look it up in your own Bible.

> *The Lord does not delay and is not tardy or slow about what He promises, according to some people's conception of slowness, but He is long-suffering (extraordinarily patient) toward you, not desiring that any should perish, but that all should turn to repentance.* (AMP)

As you begin this time of study and meditation on the truth of God's word to you, ask yourself...

> *Have I ever felt like my family and friends have given up on me?*
> *Have I ever gotten to the point where I gave up on myself?*
> *How does the above scripture make me feel when I realize God will not give up on me?*
> *Has God been extraordinarily patient towards me?*
> *What is it God wants me to do according to this scripture?*

Define the word repentance: _____

What do you need to repent of? _____

What does 1 John 1:9 tell you about how God will respond when you come to Him with true repentance? _____

_____

Write this verse out in your own words and record your thoughts and feelings about this verse in your journal. Go ahead and write out any questions you have for God. Ask Him these questions during your prayer time. When He gives you the answers, whether it is today or further along in your journey, record His answers in your journal. God is with you and wants you to begin to come to Him and rely on Him for the answers to all of your questions and concerns.

> *God has said, "Never will I leave you; never will I forsake you."* (Hebrews 13:5 NIV)

Write Hebrews 13:5 on a 3 x 5 card or put it in your phone to carry with you today. Refer to it often as you go through your day. Remember it is God's truth that will set you free today.

As you begin this day with God, thank Him for being patient with you. Thank Him for forgiving you for the unwise things you have done. Ask Him to help you to stay on course as you go through this day and remind you just how much He loves you. Thank Him for being there with you every step of the way.

Day Two: God's Incredible Faithfulness

In 1 Corinthians 10:13, God shows us just how much He wants us to succeed in this life. He not only wants us to succeed, He has promised us He will faithfully make sure we are not tempted above what we can handle. I had a very rough life, but God has brought me up and out of the street life to the cross.

> *For no temptation (no trial regarded as enticing to sin), [no matter how it comes or where it leads] has overtaken you and laid hold on you that is not common to man [that is, no temptation or trial has come to you that is beyond human resistance and that is not adjusted and adapted and belonging to human experience, and such as man can bear]. But **God is faithful [to His Word and to His compassionate nature], and He [can be trusted] not to let you be tempted and tried and assayed beyond your ability and strength of resistance and power to endure, but with the temptation He will [always] also provide the way out (the means of escape to a landing place), that you may be capable and strong and powerful to bear up under it patiently.*** (AMP emphasis added)

As you continue your journey of discovery into who God is and how much He cares for you, realize He has promised to always be there for you. You may have been abused by someone you thought you could trust, so trust is a big issue for you. God wants you to know He can be trusted. I know this is true because my trust in Him has brought me to where I am today.

Reread Romans 5:1-8 in the introduction to this week and ask yourself...

> *Who do I know that would be willing to die for me even if I was in danger because of my own choices?*

*Who actually did die for me while I was still choosing to do
things I knew were foolish or dangerous?
Why did God send Him to do this for me?*

Why can you now rejoice even when you face problems in your life?
_____

What has God given you to overcome any temptation that comes before
you? _____

As you move forward with this Bible study, God will reveal to you
all that He has placed within you to become all that He has designed and
called you to be. Remember to write your thoughts, feelings, and questions in your journal.

Write the portion of the above verse that means the most to you on a
3 x 5 card or put it in your phone to carry with you today. Refer to it often
as you go through your day. Remember it is God's truth that will set you
free today even from those things that will try to tempt you to stray from
doing things His way.

Thank God today for sending His only Son to die for you even before
you knew of His great love for you. Ask Him to begin to reveal to you all
that He has placed within you to not only withstand any temptation that
comes your way today but overcome it.

Day Three: God's Incredible Unconditional Love

God is love. *When we take up permanent residence in a life
of love, we live in God and God lives in us. This way, love
has the run of the house, becomes at home and mature in us,
so that we're free of worry on Judgment Day—our standing*

*in the world is identical with Christ's. There is no room in love for fear. Well-formed love banishes fear. Since fear is crippling, a fearful life—fear of death, fear of judgment—is one not yet fully formed in love. We, though, are going to love—love and be loved. **First we were loved, now we love. He loved us first.** (1 John 4:17-19 MSG)*

There are many scriptures in the Bible about God's love for us. We need to understand that God is love. His whole nature is to love unconditionally. He does not approve of everything we do, just like we do not approve of everything our children do. However, He never stops loving us. With this love comes the absence of fear. God does not want us to fear Him. He wants us to love Him and come to Him no matter what condition we are in. I was a drug addict and searching for love in all the wrong places when I finally came to Him and asked Him to help me escape that destructive life style.

Many times in the world, the people we love the most hurt us because their love is conditional. They love us when we are pleasing them, doing what they find acceptable, and consider good. However, some will withdraw their love or they reject us when we make poor choices or do things they do not approve of. My own family treated me this way, but God never has. He has proven to me that He loves me even when I do things He does not want me to do. Like the prodigal son in Luke 15:11-24, God still loved me and was waiting for me to run back into His loving arms.

> *Have I experienced rejection from those I love because of the choices I have made?*
> *Did this rejection and withdrawal of their love make me feel unlovable?*

How did this rejection affect my relationships with others?

Read John 3:16-17.

God so loved the world He gave _____

_____

Did God do this for you? _____

How does that make you feel? _____

Write the portions of the above verses that mean the most to you today on a 3 x 5 card or put them in your phone to carry with you today. Refer to these assurances of God's love for you often as you go through your day. Remember it is God's truth that you should believe, not what the world tells you. You are not unlovable because God loves you so much He sent His Son to save you. Walk through this day with your head held high knowing you are loved by the God of the whole universe!

Remember to add your thoughts about God's incredible love to your journal. Then pray and thank Him for this unconditional love He has for you.

Day Four: God's Incredible Promises

*My purpose in writing is simply this: that you who believe in God's Son will know beyond the shadow of a doubt that you have eternal life, the reality and not the illusion. And how bold and free we then become in his presence, freely asking according to his will, sure that he's listening. And if **we're confident that he's listening, we know that what we've asked for is as good as ours.*** (1 John 5:13-15 MSG)

Because of what Jesus did for us at the cross, we can confidently go to God and when we ask according the promises He has given us in His written word, we know He is listening and will answer our prayers. As you read in my story, God answered my prayers, though at first I did not understand because He didn't do it the way I expected.

Read Hebrews 4:16 which says we can approach God's throne through prayer with _____ and we will receive _____ and _____ in our times of need.

Hebrews 10:35-36 says you should not throw away your _____ because if you persevere you will receive _____.

Romans 4:18-21 talks about Abraham who received the promise from God even though in the eyes of the world what God had promised him should have been physically impossible.

What secret was revealed to you in verse 21 about why Abraham received his promise? _____

_____

Ask yourself...

Am I fully persuaded God has the power to do what He has promised?
Am I confident that when I pray according to God's promises that He hears and will answer my prayers?

Write out the verse that impacted you the most or put it in your phone to carry with you today. Refer to it often as you go through your day and stand on that promise know no matter what your circumstances might look like. Remember, God is listening and is well able to do what He has promised you.

Thank God today for His great and precious promises to you. Ask Him to help you stand on those promises no matter what you are facing today.

Day Five: God's Incredible Gift

> *But the free gift of grace bears no resemblance to Adam's crime that brings a death sentence to all of humanity; in fact, it is quite the opposite. For if the one man's sin brings death to so many, how much more does the gift of God's radical grace extend to humanity since Jesus the Anointed offered His generous gift. His free gift is nothing like the scourge of the first man's sin. The judgment that fell because of one false step brought condemnation, but the free gift following countless offenses results in a favorable verdict—not guilty. If one man's sin brought a reign of death—that's Adam's legacy—how much more will those who receive grace in abundance and the free gift of redeeming justice reign in life by means of one other man—Jesus the Anointed. So here is the result: as one man's sin brought about condemnation and punishment for all people, so one man's act of faithfulness makes all of us right with God and brings us to new life. Just as through one man's defiant disobedience every one of us were made sinners, so through the willing obedience*

of the one man many of us will be made right. (Romans 5:15-19 VOICE)

How would you define God's grace? _____

How did we receive the gift of God's grace? (See John 1:17) _____

What does the gift of God's grace help us do? (See Titus 2:11-12) _____

What are you to do concerning this gift from God? (See 2 Peter 3:18) _____

Without God's incredible grace, I would not be where I am today. If I had received the punishment I really deserved for the things I did, I would not be here today. God wanted me to share my story with you. His grace made a way for me to become all that He wanted me to become.

Ask Yourself...

How have I been treating this incredible gift of grace from God?

Have I been showing God how much I appreciate His love and His gift?

How can I continue to grow in the knowledge of the grace of God?

Carry the verse with that you need to refer to today to help you as you go throughout your day with confidence. Remember, grace is God's free gift to you. All you really need to do is accept it and realize how important it is to you. The truth is none of us deserve God's incredible gift of grace, but He has given us His divine assistance to live a life of godliness that fulfills His plan and purpose for us. Knowing this will set you free to be all He has called you to be today no matter what the world tries to tell you otherwise.

Thank God for His incredible gift of grace today and walk in confidence that He is going to help you accomplish great things according to His great plan and purpose for your life.

Day Six: God's Incredible Workmanship

> *You made all the delicate, inner parts of my body*
> *and knit me together in my mother's womb.*
> *Thank you for making me so wonderfully complex!*
> *Your workmanship is marvelous—how well I know it.*
> *You watched me as I was being formed in utter seclusion,*
> *as I was woven together in the dark of the womb.*
> *You saw me before I was born.*
> *Every day of my life was recorded in your book.*
> *Every moment was laid out*
> *before a single day had passed.*
> (Psalm 139:13-16 NLT)

God's incredible truth is that He personal oversaw our formation in our mother's womb. No matter the circumstances surrounding our conception, God was there and formed us the way He wanted us to be. Not one of us is a mistake. Not one of us was an accident no matter what the world might say about us. Ephesians 2:10 says, "For we are God's [own] handiwork (His workmanship), recreated in Christ Jesus, [born anew] that we may do those good works which God predestined (planned beforehand) for us [taking paths which He prepared ahead of time], that we should walk in them [living the good life which He prearranged and made ready for us to live]" (AMP).

This tells me each of us is God's own incredible workmanship. He has had a plan and a purpose for our life since before we were born. No matter what your family members say about you, it is what God says about you that it is important. The truth is God does not make mistakes. God is not random in how He forms His children. He has made each one to be unique and specially equipped to fulfill their individual purpose on this earth and no one can take their place.

How does God describe you? _____

How should you be describing yourself? _____

Have you ever been told you were an accident or unplanned? _____

Is that what God says about you? _____

Ask Yourself...

When I look in the mirror, what do I see?
What do I say to myself about myself?
How do I talk about myself to others?
Am I speaking the truth of what God says about me or am I speaking the lies others have said about me?

Write out Ephesians 2:10 in your own words. Refer to it today any time someone tries to tell you something negative about you. Refuse to believe it and tell yourself what God says about you. Remember, it is God's truth that is the only reality in your life. Everything else is a lie. Do not allow a lie to invade your thinking. God created you so He knows exactly who you are and what He designed you to be.

Thank God today for uniquely forming you and for the plan He has had for you since before you were even born. Stay focused on Him today and you can rise above any situation that comes your way.

Day Seven: God's Incredible Deliverance

> *We have everything we need to live a life that pleases God. It was all given to us by God's own power, when we learned that he had invited us to share in his wonderful goodness. God made great and marvelous promises, so that his nature would become part of us. Then we could escape our evil desires and the corrupt influences of this world.* (2 Peter 1:3-4 CEV)

If you are reading this book, you have probably been pulled into things in life that were caused by the corrupt influences of the world around you like I was. Galatians 1:3-4 says, "The Lord Jesus Christ gave himself for our sins to rescue us from this present evil age, according to the will of our God and Father" (NIV). None of us are immune to the evil corrupt influences of the world around us. The problem we run into is when we try to escape using our own strength and knowledge. This generally results in disaster as you saw as you read my story.

God the Father never expected us to try and do this on our own. He knows how the enemy will try and deceive us like he did Eve in the Garden of Eden. In 2 Corinthians 11:3, the Apostle Paul warns us about this. "But now I fear that you will be tricked, just as Eve was tricked by that lying snake" (CEV).

Our enemy is the devil and he will use various temptations to try and draw us away from serving God.

However, Psalm 3:8 says our deliverance comes from

_____.

In Matthew 6:9-13, Jesus taught us how to pray. Verse 13 says we should ask God to _____

_____.

Ask Yourself...

Have I ever tried to resist temptation by myself?
How did that work out for me?
Do I now see how I need God to be my deliverer?
Psalm 34:4 says, "I sought the Lord, and he answered me; he
_____ me from _____ my fears" (NIV).

Here is a secret about God. When He says He will deliver you from all your fears, He really means all your fears. There is no small print on this promise. All He wants you to do is trust Him and allow Him to deliver you, love you, and bless you.

Hold onto Psalm 34:4 today and refer to it often. Do not allow any temptation or fear to overtake you. Remember, though, you do not have to do this on your own. God's promise to you is that if you will trust Him, believe in what Jesus did for you on the cross, and call on His name, He will be there to see you through anything you have to face today and every day.

Thank your incredible heavenly Father for all the wonderful things you learned about Him this week. Come to Him every day and ask Him to guide you through so you can be all that He has called you to be. Next week you are going to start to learn who you are in Christ and what that means.

Week Two: Who I Am in Christ

I am the vine, and you are the branches. If you stay joined to me, and I stay joined to you, then you will produce lots of fruit. **But you cannot do anything without me.** (John 15:5 CEV emphasis added)

Jesus Christ had spent nearly three years teaching and training His disciples so they could go into the world and continue His work once God the Father called Him back to heaven. As the time grew near for Jesus to leave them, He spent more and more time preparing them for the work they would be called to do.

In fact, He told them a very amazing thing. In John 14:12-14 Jesus told them, "I tell you the truth: whoever believes in Me will be able to do what I have done, but they will do even greater things, because I will return to be with the Father. Whatever you ask for in My name, I will do it so that the Father will get glory from the Son. *Let Me say it again:* if you ask for anything in My name, I will do it" (VOICE).

Most Christians find this very hard to comprehend. Jesus healed the sick, gave sight to the blind and hearing to the deaf, raised the dead, cast out demons, and walked on water. However, if we read through the Acts of the Apostles, we will see that they did what Jesus Christ had done and even more.

Peter walked on the water and healed many people including a lame man who was begging outside the temple gates (Acts 3:1-6). When the people were amazed that he had done this he said, "Men of Israel, why does this surprise you? Why do you stare at us as if by our own power or godliness we had made this man walk? By faith in the name of Jesus, this man whom you see and know was made strong. It is Jesus' name and the faith that comes through Him that has given complete healing to him" (Acts 3:12, 16 NIV).

Whom did Peter say did the healing of the lame beggar?

_____

Later when Peter and John stood before the highly educated religious leaders and were asked to explain their actions and beliefs, these powerful leaders were astonished at their courage and knowledge though they knew the men were unschooled ordinary fishermen. They took note that these men had been with Jesus (Acts 4:13).

Acts 4:29-30 is how Peter and the other disciples prayed.

What did they ask for? _____

What happened after they prayed? _____

Read Acts 5:12-16.

What kinds of things did the disciples of Jesus Christ do in His name?

_____

As disciples of Jesus Christ, we are called to do the same. However, before we can do all of these things, we must understand who we are in Christ. Fill in the blanks with the words "in Christ Jesus" on the verses below as you prepare to learn the truth of who you are in Christ Jesus.

In the same way, count yourselves dead to sin but alive to God
_____. (Romans 6:11 NIV)

> *For the wages of sin is death, but the gift of God is eternal life*
> _____ *our Lord.* (Romans 6:23 NIV)
> *Therefore, there is now no condemnation for those who are*
> _____. (Romans 8:1 NIV)

Day One: I Am Born Again

In John 3:1-2, a Pharisee named Nicodemus came to Jesus asking how it was He could do all of the miraculous signs they had seen and heard He was doing.

What did Jesus say to this religious leader in John 3:3?
_____

What did Jesus say in John 3:7? _____

Read John 3:16-18.

What does it mean to be born again? _____

Why is this important? _____

What did Jesus come to save us from? _____

Read 2 Corinthians 5:17.

Being born again means you are a new _____ and the
_____ has _____.

Why is this so important? _____

What was your old self like? _____

Describe who you are now that you have been born again: _____
_____

Peter and John were able to do the miracles Jesus did because they were born again. You have the same power available to you. Ask God to show you who to pray for and how to pray so that He can work in and through you to help those in need all around you. As you begin to walk this out in your life, work together with a mature believer. Do not go out on your own. Jesus sent the disciples out two by two so they could work together for Him.

Record in your journal all that God reveals to you as you step out in faith to serve Him.

Remember what 2 Corinthians 5:17 says about you as you go through your day today. God's truth says because Christ has set you free, you are a new creation in Him, and have the power of God backing you up in all that you say and do.

Ask God to direct your steps today and be willing to share your testimony of God's love in your life. He will use this to begin to train you how to be this new creation in Him.

Day Two: I Am Chosen by God

> *You have not chosen Me, but **I have chosen you and I have appointed you [I have planted you]**, that you might go and bear fruit and keep on bearing, and that your fruit may be lasting [that it may remain, abide], so that whatever you ask the Father in My Name [as presenting all that I AM], He may give it to you.* (John 15:16 AMP emphasis added)

God handpicked you and "planted" you right where you are to bear fruit and keep on bearing fruit. You may have made choices that have gotten you off track, but God has been working to get you back on track so you can accomplish everything He has designed you to do. As soon as

I recognized I needed His help and asked Him to forgive me, He began to show me how He saw me, not how the world had labeled me. I did not have to live in shame any longer and neither do you.

How does that make you feel? _____

> *Even as [in His love] He **chose** us [**actually picked us out** for Himself as His own] in Christ before the foundation of the world, that we should be holy (consecrated and **set apart for Him**) and blameless in His sight, even **above reproach**, before Him in love.* (Ephesians 1:4 AMP)

Ephesians 1:4 tells you God chose you because He _____ you. God handpicked you to be set apart for Him. What does that mean? _____
Even though He knows about everything you have ever done, He sees you as _____ in His sight.
What does it mean to be above reproach? _____

Not only did God show me how He saw me, He revealed to me He had a plan and a purpose for me life. He feels the same way about you!
How does that make you feel about your future? _____

> *In Him we also were made [God's] **heritage (portion)** and we **obtained an inheritance;** for we had been foreordained (**chosen** and appointed beforehand) in accordance with **His purpose,** Who **works out everything in agreement with the counsel and design of His [own] will.*** (Ephesians 1:11 AMP)

Ephesians 1:11 says you were made as God's heritage, what does that mean to you? _____

_____

It also says you have obtained an _____.
Because God has a specific _____ for you,
He has been working everything out to agree with His
_____ for you.
How does that make you feel about yourself? _____

_____

That is why, even when I was not aware of it, God had His hand on me and was using His divine appointments to guide me where He knew I needed to be so I could achieve His purpose for me and inherit all that He had in place for me. He has a specific and specially chosen inheritance for you as well.

How has this all changed the way you see yourself?

_____

*Listen, my beloved brethren: Has not **God chosen those who are poor in the eyes of the world** to be rich in faith and in their position as believers and **to inherit the kingdom** which He has promised to those who love Him?* (James 2:5 AMP)

There are so many scriptures that prove to you God has chosen you as His own and to fulfill an important purpose in life. Choose one of them and read it to yourself as you go through your day. Remember it is God's truth that will set you free from any lies the world has told you about who you are.

Day Three: I am Created in His Image

> *God said, Let Us [Father, Son, and Holy Spirit]*
> *make mankind in **Our image, after Our likeness.***
> (Genesis 1:26 AMP)

Often people will tell us we look like one of our family members. We resemble them or we act like them. For those of us who were hurt or abused by family members, this is not always something we consider a compliment. However, as we have been learning, what God says about us is designed to lift us up and make us aware of how He sees us.

In Genesis 1:26, God says He made you in His _____.

Because of the things we have experienced in the world and the choices we have made, we may need a make-over so what God says is on the inside of us begins to affect how we look and act. The Bible refers to this as being transformed. It is a God make-over. Below are some of the scriptures that describe this God make-over. As you read them, write the highlighted words in your journal. Then use them to write a description of the newly made-over you!

> *And all of us, as with unveiled face, [because we] continued*
> *to behold [in the Word of God] as in a mirror the glory of the*
> *Lord, are constantly being **transfigured into His very own***
> ***image in ever increasing splendor** and from one degree of*
> *glory to another; [for this comes] from the Lord [Who is]*
> *the Spirit.* (2 Corinthians 3:18 AMP)

And have clothed yourselves with the new [spiritual self],
which is [ever in the process of being] renewed and remolded
*into [**fuller and more perfect knowledge upon] knowl-***
edge after the image (the likeness) of Him Who created
it. (Colossians 3:10 AMP)

Do not be conformed to this world (this age), [fashioned
after and adapted to its external, superficial customs], but
*be **transformed (changed) by the [entire] renewal of***
***your mind [by its new ideals and its new attitude]**, so*
that you may prove [for yourselves] what is the good and
acceptable and perfect will of God, even the thing which
is good and acceptable and perfect [in His sight for you].
(Romans 12:2 AMP)

As you can see from these scriptures, God is in the make-over business and He has a reason for doing it.

What did you discover was His purpose for your make-over?

_____

What has changed about your attitude toward your life?

_____

As you read through the New Testament portion of the Bible, you will discover many of the books were written by the Apostle Paul. He had one of the most amazing make-overs in the Bible. Read Acts 9:1-19.

What kind of man was Saul before he met Jesus? _____

What kind of person were you before you met Jesus? _____

Why do you think God blinded Saul as part of his make-over?

_____

Who did God send to Saul to help Him see the truth?
_____

Who did God send to you to help you see the truth? _____

What happened to Saul once this man sent by God prayed for him? _____

Read Acts 9:20-22.

What did Saul begin doing after his amazing makeover by God?
_____

How did the people who knew him respond to this new Saul?
_____

How did people who knew you respond after your God makeover? _____

What did Saul do in spite of what others said and thought about him? _____

Read Acts 9:23-25.

How do you know God was working on Saul's behalf? _____

How do you know God is working on your behalf? _____

Read Acts 9:26-30.

What happened when Saul tried to join with other believers?
_____

What did God do this time to help Saul fulfill his God-given purpose? _____

What is God doing in your life to help you fulfill your God-given purpose? _____

Saul's name was later changed to Paul. He wrote many of the things we study in the Bible. Part of his God-given purpose was to give you and me instructions through God's written word. As Paul grew in His knowledge of God as you are doing with the Bible study, he came to understand his purpose more and more. Read what he wrote in Philippians 3:10.

> *[For my determined purpose is] that I may know Him [that I may progressively become more deeply and intimately acquainted with Him, perceiving and recognizing and understanding the wonders of His Person more strongly and more clearly], and that I may in that same way come to know the power outflowing from His resurrection [which it exerts over believers], and that I may so share His sufferings as to be continually **transformed [in spirit into His likeness even]** to His death, [in the hope]* (Philippians 3:10 AMP emphasis added)

Make this your own prayer today and pray it all throughout your day. Remember it is God's truth about being transformed into His image that is important. Like Saul, you will meet those who do not believe you have changed, but God's make-over will set you free today. Watch for those special people God will send your way that will help you with your journey into His purpose for you.

Day Four: I Am Truly Free

> *In [this] freedom Christ has made us free [and completely liberated us]; stand fast then, and do not be hampered and*

held ensnared and submit again to a yoke of slavery [which
you have once put off]. (Galatians 5:1 AMP)

Ask Yourself...

> *Do I feel I am really truly free?*
> *If I do not, what still has me bound in slavery?*
> *What does Galatians 5:1 help me to understand about this*
> *yoke of slavery?*

Read John 8:36 which says, "So if the Son sets you free, you will be free
indeed" (NIV).

This says if God's Son, Jesus Christ sets **me** free then **I am**

_____.

Therefore, I no longer need to submit to _____
which is trying to once again enslave me.

This verse says I need to _____ and **I know I can
do it** because of what Jesus Christ has done for me.

In 1 Corinthians 6:11 it says, "And such some of you were [once
enslaved in sin]. But you were washed clean (purified by a complete
atonement for sin and made free from the guilt of sin), and you were consecrated (set apart, hallowed), and you were justified [pronounced righ-
teous, by trusting] in the name of the Lord Jesus Christ and in the [Holy]
Spirit of our God" (AMP).

Now, I am not only no longer a slave to sin, I have been made free
from the _____ of sin as well.

Not only that, this verse says I have been _____ to do
His work and declared _____ because of what
Jesus Christ has done in my life.

Read Galatians 3:13 which says, "Christ purchased our freedom [redeeming us] from the curse (doom) of the Law [and its condemnation] by [Himself] becoming a curse for us" (AMP).

This verse says Christ _____ my freedom.

It also says I am no longer _____ for the mistakes I have made.

Sometimes we are slaves to what other people say about us. We let them keep us locked up in how they see us instead of believing the truth about what God says about us. What Jesus did on the cross not only saved us from our sin, but also removed condemnation for it. That means God sees us as cleaned up and made-over into His image because of Jesus Christ. At first people will not see how we have been transformed. People still feared Saul even after his radical transformation, but he kept growing in the knowledge of who God said he was and he kept doing what he believed God had called him to do.

Read 1 Corinthians 7:23 which says, "A high price has been paid for your freedom, so don't devalue God's investment by becoming a slave to people" (VOICE).

Am I devaluing God's investment in me by becoming a slave
to what others say about me?
How do I need to respond to their accusations?
What do I need to do so God sees how much I do value what
Jesus Christ did for me on the cross?

You may need to take two of these verses with you today. Chose one that refers to the freedom Jesus purchased for you and then perhaps also 1 Corinthians 7:23 so you do not devalue God's investment today by believing what others may say about you. Remember it is God's truth that will set you free today and because of Jesus, you are truly free!

Thank God today for this amazing freedom and how God invested so much in you. Ask Him to help you to truly appreciate this freedom and accept all that He has for you in spite of what others may say about you. Thank God for giving you all you need to stand strong today in Him.

Day Five: I Am Truly Forgiven

> *In Him we have redemption (deliverance and salvation) through His blood, the remission (**forgiveness**) of our offenses (shortcomings and trespasses), in accordance with the riches and the generosity of His gracious favor.*
> (Ephesians 1:7 AMP)

In the New Testament portion of the Bible, the Apostle Paul wrote a letter to the Colossians in order to instruct them how to live a life that shows God how much they truly valued the investment He had made in them. Paul wanted them to grow in the knowledge of God and be clear on what Jesus Christ had done for them on the cross. He wanted their transition from the "streets" of sin to be complete so they could fulfill God's plan and purpose for their lives.

Colossian 1:14 says Jesus' work on the cross _____ you and me.

It brought us out of _____ and gave us _____ for our sins.

Colossians 2:13 says we are freely _____ for all our _____ so we are to the same for others.

What does it mean to be forgiven for your sins? _____

Read Acts 10:43. God's ways are not like the way things are done in the world. People find it hard to forgive us when we make mistakes or make wrong choices. I know many of my family and friends were like this, but God is not.

How does God say you can receive this forgiveness of all your sins?

_____

Read Matthew 18:22. God's form of forgiveness is very different than that of the world. People not only remember all our mistakes, they often keep track and when we have made the same mistake over and over they give up on us.

Is there a limit to the number of times God will forgive us of our mistakes? _____

Read Isaiah 43:25. God is not like people are when it comes to forgiveness. Not only does He forgive us, He does not keep a record of our sins once we repent and tell Him we are sorry for what we have done.

God says He forgives you for _____ sake and then He remembers yours sins _____.

Read Psalm 103:2-5, 11-2.

List the reasons you should praise the Lord for what He has done for you.

Ask Yourself...

> *Have I done what Acts 10:43 says I need to do to receive*
> *forgiveness from God?*
> *Do I believe God has truly forgiven me for all my sins?*
> *Have I forgiven myself for my past mistakes?*

Sometimes one of the hardest things to do is to forgive ourselves. When we look back over our journey through life, we are tempted to say we are a hopeless case. However, once we ask God to forgive us, we need to accept that forgiveness. If we do not, we are saying God's love and His ways apply to others but not to us. That is not what God's word says. When we say we are unforgiveable we are actually calling God a liar. He says He will forgive us. Refusing to accept His gift says to God that what Jesus did on the cross was not good enough for us.

Is that really what you want to say to God today? _____

Read Romans 3:22-24.

We _____ have sinned.

We _____ receive forgiveness for our sins through Jesus Christ.

When God says _____ He means _____. Therefore that includes _____.

There is another very important reason you need to accept God's forgiveness for yourself and realize what Jesus did on the cross was for you no matter what you have done.

In Matthew 22:37-39, Jesus said there are two great commandments we need to obey.

One is to _____ God with all your _____, _____, and _____.

The second is to _____ your neighbor as _____.

Will you be able to love others and be the witness to them God has called you to be if you cannot love and forgive yourself? _____

Pray and thank God today for truly and totally forgiving you. Remind yourself of His great love and forgiveness by memorizing Ephesians 1:7. Then ask God to show you how to forgive others even if they have not forgiven you. Ask Him to show you how to be an example of His love and forgiveness today.

Day Six: I Am a Citizen of Heaven

*Therefore you are no longer outsiders (exiles, migrants, and aliens, excluded from the rights of citizens), but you now share **citizenship** with the saints (God's own people, consecrated and set apart for Himself); and you belong to God's [own] household.* (Ephesians 2:19 AMP emphasis added)

But we are citizens of the state (commonwealth, homeland) which is in heaven, and from it also we earnestly and patiently await [the coming of] the Lord Jesus Christ (the Messiah) [as] Savior. (Philippians 3:20 AMP)

Have you ever felt like you just didn't belong? _____
Why did you feel that way? _____

Have you ever felt like an outsider? _____ Why?

_____

Have you ever felt excluded by family, classmates or neighbors? _____

Why do you feel these people treated you this way?

_____

Ephesians 2:19 say you are no longer an _____.

Philippians 3:20 also says you are a _____ of

_____.

These verses say you are a citizen of heaven because you belong to

the family of _____.

This verse also says you are entitled to the _____ of a citizen of heaven.

When you are a citizen of a country, you are granted certain rights and privileges. In the same way, as a member of God's family you have citizenship rights and privileges. Many people think they are not entitled to any of these until they die and go to heaven. However, God's word tells us something different.

In today's study of the Bible, you are going to explore what it means to be a member of God's family and a citizen of heaven while you are still living on the earth.

When Jesus walked the earth, He taught a lot about the Kingdom of Heaven. He wanted us to understand that God is our King but also our Father.

In Matthew 5:3, Jesus said those who are poor in spirit or humble are _____ because theirs is the _____

of _____.

In Matthew 6:9-10, Jesus taught us to pray. He said we are to refer to God as our _____ in _____. Then He said to pray that God's kingdom would come to _____ as it is in

_____.

Jesus was saying that God, our Father, wants us to show others why they too should desire to be citizens of heaven and members of God's own family. Often we think we are only one person and wonder how we can possibly be important in God's kingdom work.

In Matthew 13:31-32, Jesus used the parable of the mustard seed to help us see that even though we may be small, He can use us for His kingdom work.

How did reading this parable help you understand how important you are in God's kingdom? _____

_____

Many people during Jesus' time did not understand about the kingdom of God so that is why Jesus spoke so much about it to His disciples.

In Luke 17:20-21, the leaders of the church asked Jesus when the kingdom of God would come. Jesus told them that the kingdom of God was _____ them.

Jesus explained this concept again in John 3:1-7 when He told Nicodemus that he must be _____ _____ and that is how we receive the kingdom of God within us.

This concept is similar to becoming a citizen in the country of your birth. In God's kingdom, we are born again through Jesus Christ and then become rightful citizens and members of His family. In fact, we are not only citizens of heaven, we have been "adopted" into His family as sons and heirs with Christ.

Ephesians 1:5 says God adopted us as His _____ through Jesus Christ.

Romans 8:16-17 says we are God's _____ and therefore _____ within His kingdom.

When you read all of this about being a citizen of heaven and a child of God, the King, how does that make you feel? _____

_____

Remember what God says about you today and make sure you are speaking about yourself and acting like a child of the King of the kingdom of heaven. Memorize one or more of the scriptures above and refuse to believe anything less than God's truth about whose child you are.

Thank God, your heavenly Father for adopting you as His child and bringing you into citizenship in His kingdom as His child.

Day Seven: I Am Clean

Addiction means we have a compulsive need for and use of a habit-forming substance (as heroin, nicotine, or alcohol) characterized by well-defined physiological symptoms upon withdrawal; persistent compulsive use of a substance known by the user to be harmful.[2] When you have been addicted to any kind of drug, food, or habit and you go through rehabilitation, you have to become clean or cleansed not only from the effects of the drug, but then remain "sober" so that you will no longer even desire to use it.

In John 15:3, Jesus said, "Already you are clean because of the word that I have spoken to you" (ESV). Remember He said that when He sets

---

[2] © 2015 Merriam-Webster, Incorporated

us free, we are truly free. In other words, the pull or desire for the drug we are addicted to, whatever it might be, has been "cleansed" from our system.

After I realized God had answered my prayer, God delivered me not only from my addiction to drugs, He also cleansed me from any further desire for it. He gave me a greater desire and purpose in my life and truly set me free from the need or want for these destructive behaviors in my life. I had been addicted to crack cocaine from the age of twenty. I lived on the streets and was a drug addict for over seven years. I have now been sober and clean for over sixteen years. I am living proof that whom the Son sets free is free indeed!

God says if He pronounces something clean, we do not have the right to declare it unclean ever again (Acts 10:15).

Ask Yourself...

> *Has God pronounced me clean?* _____
> *How then should I refer to myself?* _____

In 1 John 1:7, it says Jesus Christ, God's Son has _____ from _____ sin and guilt. When God says all what does He mean? _____

Now that you have completed this week discovering who God says you are because of what Jesus Christ did for you on the cross, write a declaration about yourself based on His truth. Include a key phrase from each day this week in your declaration (i.e. I am forgiven because, I am clean because, I am truly free because, etc.)

Keep this declaration with you and refer to it every day. Do not let anyone or anything cause you to doubt the truth that you have discovered.

Thank God every day for His love for you. Especially thank Him for His Son, Jesus Christ and what He did for you on the cross.

Week Three: I Am Victorious

So, what do you think? With God on our side like this, how can we lose? If God didn't hesitate to put everything on the line for us, embracing our condition and exposing himself to the worst by sending his own Son, is there anything else he wouldn't gladly and freely do for us? And who would dare tangle with God by messing with one of God's chosen? Who would dare even to point a finger? The One who died for us—who was raised to life for us!—is in the presence of God at this very moment sticking up for us. Do you think anyone is going to be able to drive a wedge between us and Christ's love for us? There is no way! Not trouble, not hard times, not hatred, not hunger, not homelessness, not bullying threats, not backstabbing, not even the worst sins listed in Scripture: They kill us in cold blood because they hate you. We're sitting ducks; they pick us off one by one. None of this fazes us because Jesus loves us. I'm absolutely convinced that nothing—nothing living or dead, angelic or demonic, today or tomorrow, high or low, thinkable or unthinkable—absolutely nothing can get between us and God's love because of the way that Jesus our Master has embraced us. (Romans 8:31-39 MSG)*

The world around us will try and label us as hopeless or failures. The enemy of our souls, the devil, will lie to us and try to tell us God could never love someone as bad as we are. Even our families may declare we will never succeed at anything we try because of our past mistakes. However, as we read in Romans 8:31-37, these are all lies. God says if He is for us, who can possibly come against and win. Who can condemn or call us hopeless if God is 100 percent for our success? Since Jesus went to the cross for each and every one of us, then nothing can separate us from God's love. Just like when God says all He means all, here when He says nothing can separate us, He truly means nothing can separate us. There are no ifs, ands, or buts about it.

We are more than conquerors through His great love for us. He has given us everything we need to be victorious in our life. We may just need to gain a better understanding of all that we have at our disposal to defeat every enemy or every kind. We have the victory through Christ because God says so. If God said it, we can trust it and believe it! I am living proof that this is true!

> *Thanks be to God, Who gives us the victory [making us conquerors] through our Lord Jesus Christ.* (1 Corinthians 15:57 AMP)

Day One: I am Armed and Ready

> *But no weapon that is formed against you shall prosper, and every tongue that shall rise against you in judgment you shall show to be in the wrong. This [peace, righteousness, security, triumph over opposition] is the heritage of the servants of the Lord [those in whom the ideal Servant of the Lord is reproduced]; this is the righteousness or the vindication which they obtain from Me [this is that which I impart to them as their justification], says the Lord.* (Isaiah 54:17 AMP)

Here is another awesome promise from God. Not only is He 100 percent for our success in life, He has fully equipped us to handle any attack from the enemy that comes against us. We need to remember that our enemy, the devil, is a liar. We can always defeat this enemy with the truth. Jesus showed us just how to do this when the devil tried to trick Him and defeat Him.

In Matthew 4:1-11, we see the devil dared to try and tempt Jesus to believe his lies instead of standing on the truth. I believe God showed us this so we could see just how God would like us to handle this enemy.

First of all, in verses 1-4, the devil came to Jesus when He was _____ and _____.

Yes, Jesus was a man even though He was God's Son. The temptation the devil used here was aimed at Jesus' weakened condition. One of the main tactics of the devil is to come at us when we are vulnerable. He will tempt us to be willing to give up everything for what we are addicted to.

That is definitely how the devil came after me. I would begin to gain strength when I was in jail and regularly read my Bible, but when I got back out on the street where I was vulnerable, the doubts and fears crept back in to lure me back into the enemy's snare.

In Matthew 4:4, Jesus shows us how to get the devil off our back when he tries to tempt us in this way. He quoted Deuteronomy 8:3 from God's written word. You and I can use this same method to send the devil on his way. When we tell the devil what God says in His written word, the devil cannot argue with us.

> *Jesus told him, "No! The Scriptures say, 'People do not live by bread alone, but by every word that comes from the mouth of God.'" (NLT)*

The second way the devil tried to tempt Jesus was to put God to the test and see if God really means what He says in His word (Matthew 4:5-6). In other words, if the enemy can get us to _____ that God really means what He says, then we cannot receive that promise.

Jesus came back at the devil with another verse of scripture, this time Jesus quoted Deuteronomy 6:16 when He said, "The Scriptures also say, 'You must _____ _____ the LORD your God'" (Matthew 4:7 NLT).

The third and final temptation was in the area of _____. Unfortunately, many people today will bargain with the devil in order to attain _____ and _____.

They do not realize what a liar and a cheat the devil really is and when they do business with this enemy, destruction is where they are headed. Jesus quoted Deuteronomy 6:13 to finally send the devil on his way (Matthew 4:10-11).

The only way we can do battle this way is make sure we study the written word of God which is the Bible. The more scriptures we have learned and memorized, the easier it will be to defeat this tricky foe.

Ephesians 6:17 calls the word of God our most powerful weapon; it is our _____.

Hebrews 4:12 says the word of God is sharper than _____. This means it can easily cut through the lies of the _____.

2 Timothy 2:15 says we are to study the _____ of _____ and correctly handle the _____ of _____. That is because we know the word of truth is the way to _____ in Christ.

Ask Yourself...

Has the enemy tried to confuse or trick me through my weaknesses or through doubting God's promises?_____
Was I able to withstand the lies and tricks of the enemy?_____
Have I studied the written word of God so that I now know how to use it as a weapon against the lies and tricks of the enemy?_____

No soldier ever goes into battle without knowing how to use the weapons he or she has been given to fight with against the enemy. We need to know how to use the powerful sword God has given us to send the enemy running. I began to learn this powerful truth while I was in jail. Unfortunately, I did not understand how important it was to study and use the word of truth as a weapon against the enemy's lies and deceptions. Now I do and I make study of the written word of God part of my every day routine to stay alert and ready to stand firm and cause him to flee in the name of Jesus Christ.

So humble yourselves before God. Resist the devil, and he will flee from you. (James 4:7 NLT)

Remember it is God's word of _____ that gives you the sword you need to defeat your enemy and the deceptive tricks he will use to try and keep you bound. It is the truth of God through knowing and using His written word that will set you free and send the enemy on his way today.

When doubts or thoughts that you know are from the enemy begin to invade your mind, quote the verses you have been studying and memorizing. When you do, he has to flee! He knows he cannot win against the word of God!

Thank God today for the powerful weapons He has given you to withstand the attacks of the enemy.

Day Two: I have the Full Armor of God

Be strong in the Lord and in his mighty power. **Put on all of God's armor so that you will be able to stand firm against all strategies of the devil.** *For we are not fighting against flesh-and-blood enemies, but against evil rulers and authorities of the unseen world, against mighty powers in this dark world, and against evil spirits in the heavenly places. Therefore, put on every piece of God's armor so you will be able to resist the enemy in the time of evil. Then after the battle you will still be standing firm.* (Ephesians 6:10-13 NLT)

In our last lesson, we talked about the weapons God has provided for us to do battle against the devil. We saw that His word was what Jesus used to do battle against the temptations the enemy tried to bring against Him. This powerful passage in the book of Ephesians tells us God has not only given us a sword to do battle with, He has equipped us with full body armor.

We need this full body armor in order to _____ _____ against the _____ of the devil.

If we put on every piece of the body armor God has given we are equipped to _____ the _____.

What this tells us is that when we become a citizen of God's kingdom, we are also joining His heavenly army. The fact that He has equipped us to stand firm against the enemy means God knows the enemy is going to come after us just like he did Jesus. The good news is God will never allow us to go into battle without the proper body armor and weapons to insure our victory.

Just like any good soldier though, we need to be properly trained in how to use this armor effectively. So today's lesson is in understanding the various pieces of the armor and learning how to properly use them.

First of all, Ephesians 6:14 says to stand firm with the belt of _____ buckled around your waist.

We have already studied how important knowing God's truth is against the enemy's lies. Soldiers have a utility belt that keeps their weapons and ammunition always handy for battle. In our fight against the devil, our main weapon is God's truth.

> How would you explain the value of having God's truth as your most powerful weapon against the enemy to someone else who is facing some of the challenges you have? _____
> _____

Secondly, it also says we are to cover our upper body with the bullet proof body armor called the breastplate of _____ which protects our _____.

> Every enemy knows if he can land a weapon in the_____, he can kill the soldier.
> In our warfare against the devil, he will also seek to damage our
> _____.

The best way to protect our hearts is to seek first God's kingdom and seek to do things His way. When we do then the enemy has a hard time getting a foothold in our lives. When we try to do things in our own way and in our own strength, we leave ourselves unprotected and vulnerable.

I did that so many times when I was living on the street and I got myself in trouble time and time again.

Staying within the parameters of His right way of doing battle keeps us protected from a frontal attack. Thank God He always has our back!

Have you ever been tempted to compromise what you know was right? _____

Do you see now it could have been a subtle attack of the enemy to get you to lose your integrity and get you into trouble? _____

What will you do differently next time? _____

Thirdly, read Ephesians 6:15. No soldier will head into battle without proper _____.

It is hard to march across the ground if our feet are not properly protected. Wearing military boots means our feet, ankles, and even our shins are fully protected. If the enemy can knock our feet out from under us, he can take us down.

Ephesians 6:15 says one of the enemy's most subtle ways of trying to knock our feet out from under us is to steal our _____.

As we have learned, our only true peace comes from knowing who God is, how much He loves us, and forgives us no matter who we are or what we have done. This is called the gospel or good news of peace because of what Jesus did for us on the cross. The only way I could get out of life on the street was to believe in the good news of what Jesus did for me on the cross.

Have you ever felt like your feet were knocked out from under you? _____

What happened to cause you to feel this way?_____

How can you guard against this in the future?_____

Fourth, Ephesians 6:16 says we need to also take up the _____ of _____.

It says we need this in order to _____ the _____ _____ of the evil one who is of course the devil.

This shows us that the enemy has many weapons and strategies to use against us and we need to be alert and prepared to meet all of them. The devil does not fight fair. He will use whatever he can to hurt and destroy us. He will even use those we care about to "burn us" with their words and actions. Betrayal and rejection are fiery darts and lethal arrows he will shoot at us sometimes using those closest to us to cause us great pain and keep us from gaining the victory.

Several times I thought I had found someone I could trust and be with the rest of my life. When they betrayed me and cheated on me, it caused a deep wounding that nearly took me out of the battle. I became depressed and nearly gave up because of these fiery arrows.

Have you ever had a close friend or loved one betray you? _____

Who betrayed Jesus in Matthew 26:47-50 and caused Him to be arrested? _____

Who even denied they knew Jesus when He needed this close friend the most in Matthew 26:69-75? _____

Does Jesus know how we feel? _____ Can we go to Him with this hurt? _____

Fifth, we are to put on the helmet of _____ (Ephesians 6:17).

Why do soldiers wear a helmet? _____

Read Proverbs 23:7 which says what a person _____ about is what they become.

Read Philippians 4:8 which gives you a list of positive things to _____ about.

Read 2 Corinthians 10:5 which says we are to take every _____ captive.

Everything we say or do begins with a thought. The devil cannot make us do anything, but he can try to get us to accept his negative, destructive lies into our thoughts. The mind is where the enemy really begins his battle to control us. If we know how much God loves us, we know who God says we are, and believe all of His promises are true, then we will not be tempted to believe the devil's lies.

What is the helmet of salvation protecting you from?

_____

Right now tell the enemy how much God loves you, who God says you are, and tell him the promise you are standing on against his lies. Do this daily to protect your mind and your thoughts. Determine to take every thought captive today and every day.

So along with the sword to use as your defensive and offensive weapon, you have what you need to stand against the devil's schemes. As you go through each day, picture Jesus standing behind you, covering your back and marching with you to face anything you might come up against today.

Thank God for your heavenly armor and all that He has given you to not only withstand the attacks, but defeat your enemy and send him running.

Day Three: I am an Overcomer

> *In the world you have tribulation and trials and distress and frustration; but be of good cheer [take courage; be confident, certain, undaunted]! For **I have overcome the world**. [I have deprived it of power to harm you and have conquered it for you.]* (John 16:33 AMP emphasis added)

To overcome something means to prevail over and gain superiority over it. It doesn't rule you or influence you, you rule over and influence it.

Would you describe yourself as an overcomer? _____

What have you been able to overcome in life? _____

What have you had trouble overcoming in your life?

_____

What do you think you need to do to overcome this area of your life? _____

Revelation 12:11 says the people of God overcame the devil by believing in and standing on what Christ did on the cross and by the words of their own _____.

In other words, they were willing to tell others what Christ had done for them.

1 John 4:4 it also says the reason they could overcome the agents of the devil is because of the power and strength of _____ _____ that lives with us. It says this is greater than the power and strength of the one who is in the world, the _____.

Romans 12:21 tells us not to let ourselves be _____, but we are to _____ evil with _____.

One of the ways I believe God has led me to begin overcoming evil with good in my life is by writing this book and sharing my testimony as a motivational speaker.

How do you think you can begin overcoming evil with good in your life? _____

Ask Yourself...

Have I ever wondered why I experience trials, tribulations, and troubles? _____

Have I wondered if I am I doing something wrong to cause them? _____

Have I ever asked God why me? _____

We often wonder why it is we must go through hard times and wilderness experiences in our lives. In Deuteronomy 8:2-5, God led His people into the wilderness so they would discover what was in their own hearts and minds especially concerning their relationship with God. They needed to know for themselves that when times get tough, they would still chose to obey Him. Sometimes that is why God has us go through our wilderness times as well.

Sometimes what we are going through is because of the choices we have made and have gone against God's ways and we need to learn the hard way why God tells us to do things His way. God also wants us to learn more about ourselves and about Him. He wants to show us we can be strong in the face of trials and tribulations because He has personally equipped us to be overcomers.

What have you learned about yourself as you have gone through your tough times?

What have you learned about God? _____

_____

I had very good intentions while I was in jail and reading the Bible and praying. However, once I was back out in the world, I did not have the strength to withstand the attacks and temptations of the enemy. God knew I needed to learn more about Him and about me so I could truly live the abundant prosperous life He had in store for me. Every time I spent time in jail after another "wilderness" time in the world, I became stronger and stronger until finally I had the knowledge and the strength to really commit my life to Him, once and for all.

Now I cannot wait to share my testimony with others. I know the more I share my testimony with others the stronger I become.

> *In the Messiah, in Christ, God leads us from place to place in one perpetual victory parade. Through us, he brings knowledge of Christ. Everywhere we go, people breathe in the exquisite fragrance. Because of Christ, we give off a sweet scent rising to God, which is recognized by those on the way of salvation.* (2 Corinthians 2:14 MSG)

Take a few minutes and write out a brief testimony that you can share with others about your time in the wilderness and how God brought you through it. Keep it short enough that you can share it in three minutes or less. Then practice it so you have it handy whenever God sends you someone who needs to hear it.

_____

God wants us to be overcomers. He wants to bless us with all the blessings or heaven. He also wants us to share our testimony with others so they too can receive all that He has for them.

Thank God today that He is teaching you how to become an overcomer. Ask Him to show you how you can use your testimony to help others.

Day Four: I Will Run the Race to Win

> *Don't you realize that in a race everyone runs, but only one person gets the prize? So run to win!* (1 Corinthians 9:24 NLT)

Philippians 3:14 explains, we should not only run the race, but

_____.

Why? _____

Hebrews 12:1 gives us a plan for how to run this race, finish it, and win.

1. Let us strip off every _____ that slows us down.
2. This means to stop the _____ that so easily trips us up.
3. Then run with _____ the race God has set before us.

If you have ever trained for a marathon or any kind of race, you know that one of the key factors is building up endurance. Many people start out really strong and fast, but they cannot make it to the end.

Why do you think that is? _____

What do you have to do to build up endurance in this race against sin and temptation? _____

The Apostle Paul had a young disciple he was training to take over leading one of the local churches. He gave this man some advice that will help us in our race of life as well.

2 Timothy 1:8 says not to be _____ to _____ about the Lord Jesus Christ.

Ask yourself, can this be said about me? _____

Why or why not? _____

2 Timothy 2:3 says to endure _____ like a good _____.

Ask yourself, am I behaving like a good soldier for Jesus Christ? _____

Why or why not? _____

2 Timothy 2:4 says not to get involved in _____ affairs, but instead to _____ your commanding officer. Who is your commanding officer? _____

Ask yourself, is what I am doing pleasing my commanding officer? _____

Why or why not? _____

2 Timothy 2:5 says like an athlete who wants to win, compete according to the _____.

Ask yourself, am I competing according to God's rules? _____

Why or why not? _____

2 Timothy 2:15 instructs us to correctly handle the _____ of _____.

Ask yourself, would God approve of my workmanship? _____

Why or why not? _____

2 Timothy 2:16 warns us to avoid _____ _____.

Ask yourself, can this be said of me? _____

Why or why not? _____

2 Timothy 2:22 instructs us to flee the _____ _____ of youth.

Ask yourself, am I successfully doing this? _____

Why or why not? _____

Instead we are to pursue _____, _____, _____,

and _____.

Ask yourself, am I pursuing these things? _____

Why or why not? _____

2 Timothy 2:23 tells us not to have anything to do with _____

_____.

Ask yourself, am I avoiding foolish arguments? _____

Do I cause or stop quarrels? _____

2 Timothy 2:24 says we must not _____.

Instead we are to be _____ to _____.

Ask yourself, am I kind to everyone? _____

Am I resentful? _____

Am I able to teach others the way God would have me teach?

_____

2 Timothy 2:25-26 says the way I teach others is important because ____

_____

What is keeping me from gently instructing others?

_____

What does 2 Timothy 3:16-17 tell us we need to do to be thoroughly equipped for every good work? _____

Ask Yourself...

Am I ready to run this race to win? _____

*Am I willing to do what it takes to endure to the end?*_____

*Will I continually read through the scriptures so I can be fully equipped for every good work?*_____

*Will I strive to be the witness for Christ God has called me to be?*_____

Use the list of verses from Paul's advice to Timothy as your check list. Go back and circle the ones you need to work on so you can run this race and win.

Put together a "training plan" to get yourself in shape to run, endure, and win.

Like many athletes need to do, get yourself a coach who is strong in the things of God and can help you become stronger and will hold you accountable to your training plan.

I thank God for the Salvation Army "training program" I became a part of. I thank God for my "friend" who held me accountable and made sure I attended all the meetings and stayed sober. Because I submitted to this training program, I can now help others run their race as well.

The Apostle Paul was training Timothy to go on and train others and help them prepare for their own races. We are called to do the same. Which of the above verses will help you the most to run your race successfully today. Keep it with you, refer to it often, and run to win today.

Thank God for the "coach" and the "training program" He has sent your way. Ask Him to help you stay committed to completing your training and then to run your race to win.

Day Five: I am Fearless

> *For God did not give us a spirit of timidity or cowardice or*
> *fear, but [He has given us a spirit] of power and of love and*
> *of sound judgment and personal discipline [abilities that*
> *result in a calm, well-balanced mind and self-control].* (2
> Timothy 1:7 AMP)

> *So what should we say about all of this? If God is on our side,*
> *then tell me: whom should we fear?* (Romans 8:31 VOICE)

I cannot even tell you how many times someone said to me, "Misty, I have got your back. Misty, you do not have to be afraid. I will be there for you." Sometimes, I could count on them, but many times if something came along that meant more to them than I did, they were not so trustworthy. In fact, the longer I was on the street, the more fearful I became. At first things were fun and exciting. I felt so much freer than the life I was living at home where I was constantly the victim of the men around me. At first I felt invincible. Then I began to learn the things to fear.

There were men out there that sought to do me harm. There were drugs out there that could take me to a place I might never come back from. The devil had a destructive plan for me life as well. Though he offered me an escape from reality, I began to see just how high the cost would eventually be and it frightened me.

Ask Yourself...

> *What have I been afraid of in the past?*_____

*Have there been those who have said they were there for me, but when it came down to it, they left me alone to face my fears?*_____
How can I now help others learn to trust God so they no longer need to be afraid? _____

_____

Day Six: I am Wise

Do you want to be counted wise, to build a reputation for wisdom? Here's what you do: Live well, live wisely, live humbly. It's the way you live, not the way you talk, that counts. Mean-spirited ambition isn't wisdom. Boasting that you are wise isn't wisdom. Twisting the truth to make yourselves sound wise isn't wisdom. It's the furthest thing from wisdom—it's animal cunning, devilish conniving. Whenever you're trying to look better than others or get the better of others, things fall apart and everyone ends up at the others' throats.

Real wisdom, God's wisdom, *begins with a holy life and is characterized by getting along with others. It is gentle and reasonable, overflowing with mercy and blessings, not hot one day and cold the next, not two-faced. You can develop a healthy, robust community that lives right with God and enjoy its results only if you do the hard work of getting along with each other, treating each other with dignity and honor.*
(James 3:13-18 MSG)

Wisdom is knowledge combined with understanding. If we read the Bible but do not understand how it applies to our everyday life, it will not give us the wisdom we need to live in a godly productive way.

Look at the first part of the scripture passage above and list what wisdom is not.

1. _____
2. _____
3. _____
4. _____

Ask Yourself...

Have I done any of these things trying to look wise in the eyes of others? _____

How has that worked out for me? _____

Look at the second part of the scripture passage above and describe what godly wisdom really is.

1. _____
2. _____
3. _____
4. _____

Ask Yourself...

Is this how others would describe the wisdom I display in my life? _____

If not, what do I need to work on to exhibit real, godly wisdom? _____

The book of James gives us a lot of information on how to begin to exhibit real, godly wisdom.

James 1:5 says if we lack wisdom we need to _____.

James 1:6 also says we must _____ and not _____ when we ask for this godly wisdom.

James 1:7 says a person who asks God for wisdom, but then doubts will not _____.

James 1:8 calls this person _____ and _____.

How would you define someone who is double-minded and unstable?

_____

Ask Yourself...

> *When I pray and ask God for wisdom to handle a situation, does my prayer sound like I believe I will receive or doubt He will help me?*_____
>
> *Do my words and actions show I am unstable and double-minded?*_____
>
> *What do I need to do change?* _____

Read the parable Jesus taught in Matthew 7:24-27.

What did Jesus say you need to do to become truly wise?

_____

We have already discovered the best place to find out God's way to do things is by reading the Bible. Most Bibles have a section in the back where you can look up key words and find verses that relate to that subject. Look up the word "wise" or "wisdom" and then read each of the verses listed.

Write what you learn from each verse and then choose the one you feel you need to have with you today.

Remember, 2 Timothy 3:16 says, "**Every Scripture** is God-breathed (given by His inspiration) and profitable for instruction, for reproof *and* conviction of sin, for correction of error *and* discipline in obedience, [and] for training in righteousness (in holy living, in conformity to God's will in thought, purpose, and action)" (AMP emphasis added).

You can use this same method to research any subject or issue you need to study to increase in godly knowledge and understanding. It is particularly effective if you work together with a study partner so you can discuss together what you have discovered

> *Walk with the **wise** and become **wise**, for a companion of fools suffers harm.* (Proverbs 13:20 NIV)

This is another lesson I learned the hard way. I did not choose my companions wisely. It really does make a difference who we spend our time with on a regular basis. Our language and our behavior will become like those we spend the most time with. We need to choose our friends wisely.

Ask Yourself...

What are some of the behaviors I would like to change in my life? _____

Do I see these behaviors in the people I spend most of my time with? _____

Is God asking me to make some changes in the friends I spend most of my time with? _____

Will I do it now that know how important it is? _____

115

Thank God today for His written word, the Bible, that helps you increase in knowledge and understanding. Ask Him to show you the path to true godly wisdom in all your choices today. Thank Him for godly friends and ask Him to show you who you need to pull back from spending so much time with.

Remember, His ways are always aimed at making you wiser and more productive in your life.

Day Seven: I will Use My Gifts and Talents

> [Jesus] said, "A nobleman was called away to a distant empire to be crowned king and then return. Before he left, he called together ten of his servants and divided among them ten pounds of silver, saying, 'Invest this for me while I am gone.' After he was crowned king, he returned and called in the servants to whom he had given the money. He wanted to find out what their profits were. The first servant reported, 'Master, I invested your money and made ten times the original amount!' 'Well done!' the king exclaimed. 'You are a good servant. You have been faithful with the little I entrusted to you, so you will be governor of ten cities as your reward.' The next servant reported, 'Master, I invested your money and made five times the original amount.' 'Well done!' the king said. 'You will be governor over five cities.' But the third servant brought back only the original amount of money and said, 'Master, I hid your money and kept it safe. I was afraid because you are a hard man to deal with, taking what isn't yours and harvesting crops you didn't plant.' 'You wicked servant!' the king roared. 'Your

own words condemn you. If you knew that I'm a hard man who takes what isn't mine and harvests crops I didn't plant, why didn't you deposit my money in the bank? At least I could have gotten some interest on it.' Then, turning to the others standing nearby, the king ordered, 'Take the money from this servant, and give it to the one who has ten pounds.' 'But, master,' they said, 'he already has ten pounds!' 'Yes,' the king replied, 'and to those who use well what they are given, even more will be given. But from those who do nothing, even what little they have will be taken away.'" (Luke 19:12-27 NLT)

Jesus often taught using parables which were little short stories with a lesson He was trying to explain to His listeners. He used examples of things that could be happening in their lives so they could relate to these lessons in a practical way.

In the parable above, Jesus was teaching about the abilities and talents God has placed within us using silver as an example of what He has given us. We have already learned that God designed us for a specific purpose as we were being formed in our mother's womb. He has placed within us everything we need to be able to accomplish His plan and purpose for our lives.

However, we have a part to play in this as well. God expects us to discover, develop, and use those talents to live a productive life and bless others as He has blessed us. He expects a return on His investment.

As you read the parable above, what did the master say to those who used the talents they were given to produce even more? ____

What did the master say to one who just hid that "talent" and did nothing with it?_____

This same parable is also recorded in Matthew 25:14-30. In this version, however, Jesus said the man going on a journey distributed the talents a little differently.

Verse 15 says, "To one He gave _____, to another _____, and to the third servant _____, each according to his _____" (NIV).

Often the world will tell us we do not have any talent or that we will never amount to anything. God's truth tells us this is not true. The truth is He has given each of us the talent we need to accomplish our specific purpose.

One of the men I thought would love and care for me ended up abusing me and telling me I was useless, a nobody, and how lucky I was he would even marry me. At that point I did not know I was a child of God and that even though I had not finished high school, He had a plan and purpose for my life. I believed the lie then, but now the truth has set me free and I am using the abilities and talents God placed within me to run my own successful business as well as to reach out and help others.

Has anyone ever told you that you would never amount to anything?_____
Did a teacher or a fellow student ever call you stupid or ignorant?_____
What does God's truth say about you?_____
Who should you believe?_____

There is another parable Jesus told about producing a harvest from what we have learned from God's written word.

A farmer went out to plant his seed. As he scattered it across his field, some seed fell on a footpath, where it was stepped on, and the birds ate it. Other seed fell among rocks. It began to grow, but the plant soon wilted and died for lack of moisture. Other seed fell among thorns that grew up with it and choked out the tender plants. Still other seed fell on fertile soil. This seed grew and produced a crop that was a hundred times as much as had been planted!" When he had said this, he called out, "Anyone with ears to hear should listen and understand." His disciples asked him what this parable meant. "This is the meaning of the parable: The seed is God's word. The seeds that fell on the footpath represent those who hear the message, only to have the devil come and take it away from their hearts and prevent them from believing and being saved. The seeds on the rocky soil represent those who hear the message and receive it with joy. But since they don't have deep roots, they believe for a while, then they fall away when they face temptation. The seeds that fell among the thorns represent those who hear the message, but all too quickly the message is crowded out by the cares and riches and pleasures of this life. And so they never grow into maturity. And the seeds that fell on the good soil represent honest, good-hearted people who hear God's word, cling to it, and patiently produce a huge harvest. (Luke 8:5-15)

What did the seed in this parable represent? _____

Was there any difference in the seed that landed in the various soils? _____

What then caused some of the seed to produce a great crop while other seed did not?_____
Which kind of "soil" are you? _____
How does using the seed to produce a harvest relate to using your God-given talents and abilities? _____
How do you know God expects you to produce a "harvest" from the good seed that He has planted within you? _____
_____

There is one more parable Jesus taught that also relates to using all the gifts, knowledge, talents, and abilities God has made available to us.

> *"No one lights a lamp and then covers it with a bowl or hides it under a bed. A lamp is placed on a stand, where its light can be seen by all who enter the house. For all that is secret will eventually be brought into the open, and everything that is concealed will be brought to light and made known to all. So pay attention to how you hear. To those who listen to my teaching, more understanding will be given. But for those who are not listening, even what they think they understand will be taken away from them."* (Luke 8:16-18 NLT)

This time Jesus compared what God has provided for us as what?
_____
What did you learn from this parable? _____

I believe God has called me to let my light shine by sharing my testimony of all that He has done in my life and how He brought me from the streets to the cross and then to having my own successful company. Only God could have done this in and through me. If He did it for me, He will surely do it for you as well.

Ask Yourself...

> *What special talents or abilities has God placed within me?*_____
> *What do I need to do to further develop them so I can produce a good harvest?*_____
> *Am I continually planting His good seed in myself by daily reading His written word, the Bible?*_____
> *Am I sharing my "light" with others by being willing to talk about all that God has done in my life?*_____

Pray and ask God to give you the courage to move forward and develop the gifts, talents, and abilities He has placed within you. Remember to believe what God says about you and not what others have labeled you.

> *Jesus replied, "What is impossible with man is possible with God." (Luke 18:27 NIV)*

Week Four: My Call

> *[Urged on] by faith Abraham, when he was **called, obeyed** and went forth to a place which he was destined to receive as an inheritance; and he went, although he did not know or trouble his mind about where he was to go. (Hebrews 11:8 AMP emphasis added)*

In the Old Testament portion of the Bible which was written before the birth of Jesus Christ, a man named Abraham was called by God to leave his homeland and go to a land God would lead him to. This man had no idea where God was calling him to go, but he had an amazing promise from God if he would answer this call (Genesis 12:1-4). Abraham answered the call and God blessed him, his family, and all the people of the earth were blessed through him!

We have also been called by God to fulfill His plan and purpose for our lives. We have already learned God will keep His promises if we keep up our end of the agreement.

> *[For it is He]* ***Who delivered and saved us and called us*** *with a calling in itself holy and leading to holiness [to a life of consecration, a vocation of holiness]; [He did it] not because of anything of merit that we have done, but because of and* ***to further His own purpose and grace*** *(unmerited favor) which was given us in Christ Jesus before the world began [eternal ages ago].* (2 Timothy 1:9 AMP emphasis added)

What is the amazing promise we are given in Romans 8:28?

_____

Are you ready to move forward and begin to learn about and fulfill your call this week? _____

Open your heart and mind to receive all that God has for you this week!

Day One: Salt of the Earth

You are the salt of the earth, but if salt has lost its taste (its strength, its quality), how can its saltiness be restored? It is not good for anything any longer but to be thrown out and trodden underfoot by men. (Matthew 5:13 AMP)

Ephesians 4:1 says we are to lead a life worthy of our _____.

According to Matthew 5:13 that includes being the _____ of the earth.

Some of the common uses of salt are to preserve _____, _____, and add _____ to food.

The point of this analogy, though, is that if salt loses its strength and quality, it is no longer good for anything. It can no longer serve its true purpose.

The same is true for us as members of God's kingdom family. He never meant for us to just sit around and do nothing. We have a very unique and specific purpose in life just like salt has a very unique and specific purpose.

Often our unique and specific purpose has to do with what we are really good at, for example sports or business administration. God expects us to function as His representative doing what we are really good at.

What are you really good at? _____

Once I was given the chance to work, I found out I was really good at being a supervisor in the cleaning business. I was so good at my job that I eventually was able to open and run my own company. My company has become such a blessing that I have now been able to hire seven other people and give them jobs as well. I believe this is how God has helped me become the salt of the earth in my area of influence.

Another way to identify what our unique and specific purpose might be is to find out how what we are really good at can help others and fulfill a need in our community.

How can you use what you are really good at to help in your community? _____

For example, if you are good at sports perhaps you can volunteer at a local girls or boys club and coach young people. Most local community activities and events can use volunteers in a variety of capacities from set up to clean up afterwards. You just need to check it out and see how you can be salt to your community.

"Let me tell you why you are here," says Jesus. "You're here to be salt-seasoning that brings out the God-flavors of this earth. If you lose your saltiness, how will people taste godliness? You've lost your usefulness and will end up in the garbage" (Matthew 5:13 MSG).

Jesus was teaching His disciples that what they do with the talents and gifts God has given them profoundly affects the world around them. He cautioned them to not do anything that might compromise this influence. In this way, salt refers to a Christian's character.

Romans 5:3-4 reminds us that some of the trials and tribulations we go through are to _____ our character.

1 Corinthians 15:33 warns us _____ _____ corrupts good character.

This means we need to choose our _____ wisely.

This was an area I had to work hard at perfecting. I truly needed the wisdom of God to help me know who I should have as trusted friends and who would not be a good influence on me, especially during my early months of seeking to do things God's way and not the world's way.

As we have learned, God does not tell us to do something like be the salt of the earth without instructing us how to do it. He never asks us to do something He has not provided a way for us to accomplish it. He has given us His written word to teach us how to do live a life that draws others to Him.

James 4:17 warns us if we know the _____ we _____ do and do not do it, we _____.

Matthew 7:12 says in everything we do we should treat _____ like we want to be _____.

1 Corinthians 10:24 says no one should seek their own _____ but seek the _____ of _____.

1 Corinthians 10:31-32 instructs us to do everything we do to _____ God so that we do not cause anyone else to _____.

1 Corinthians 10:33 further instructs us to not seek our own _____ by to try to seek the _____ of others and to _____ everyone in _____ way.

Proverbs 18:21 says our tongues have the power of _____ and _____. This means we should be careful of what we say because our words can help or hurt others.

Galatians 6:2 says we should _____ each other's _____. In other words, if we know someone else needs help, we should do what we can to help and not expect someone else to help them.

Galatians 6:10 says we should take every opportunity to do _____ to _____. This means we do not necessarily wait for someone to come and ask us for help. Most of us do not feel comfortable doing that. If we keep our eyes and hearts open, God will show us who it is He wants us to help.

Use this list of instructions from God to begin to train yourself to be the salt of the earth.

Ask Yourself...

Do I do what I know is right so that others can see the strength God has given me?____

Do I treat others the way I want them to treat me?_____

Do I try to please others with what I do and seek their good over mine?_____

Do I help or hurt others with my words?_____

Do I really look for opportunities to help others?_____

And let us not lose heart and grow weary and faint in acting nobly and doing right, for in due time and at the appointed season we shall reap, if we do not loosen and relax our courage and faint. (Galatians 6:9 AMP)

Day Two: Light of the World

*You are the **light of the world**. A city set on a hill cannot be hidden. Nor do men light a lamp and put it under a peck measure, but on a lampstand, and it gives light to all in the house. **Let your light so shine before men that they may see your moral excellence and your praiseworthy, noble, and good deeds and recognize and honor and praise and***

glorify your Father Who is in heaven. (Matthew 5:14-16
AMP emphasis added)

Jesus wanted to make very sure we understood what He wants us to do as productive members of the kingdom of God. The instructions He gives as to how we are to be the light of the world refer to our character.

Others are to see our light shine by our _____ _____ and our _____, _____, and _____ _____.

> What does it mean to have moral excellence? _____
> Describe a praiseworthy deed you have done: _____
> Think of a noble deed you could do in your neighborhood or at your job: _____
> In John 8:12, Jesus tells us He is the _____ of the _____. Therefore, for us to let our light shine we must _____ Him.

There was a phrase that has been used to help us as we make godly decisions in our daily walk. WWJD means we need to stop and ask ourselves, What Would Jesus Do in this situation. If we model our actions after His, we will be the light of the world He wants us to be. Here are a few examples from the scriptures to help you begin to let your light shine by discovering what Jesus would do in a specific situation. There are many more you will discover as you read your Bible. List them in your journal as you read more about Jesus' life and ministry.

> How did Jesus treat the woman caught in adultery in John 8:3-5, 7, 9-11? _____
> How did He treat the Samaritan woman at the well in John 4:4-26?
> _____

What did Jesus say to do about those who make fun of your faith in Matthew 5:43-45? _____

Jesus also taught on the idea of revenge in Matthew 5:38-39. How did He say we should handle it? _____

What does Jesus say about forgiving those who have sinned against us in Matthew 6:14-15? _____

How did Jesus say we should handle worry in Matthew 6:25-34?
_____

How do you think your friends and neighbors are going to respond when they see you refusing to live in worry all the time no matter what is happening around you? _____

Is this a good way to let your light shine before men so they will see the value of doing things God's way? _____

The Apostle Paul prayed for those who were seeking to let their light shine before men in Ephesians 1:18. Personalize this and make it your prayer today as well.

> *By having the eyes of* [**My**] *heart flooded with light, so that* [**I**] *can know and understand the hope to which He has called* [**Me**], *and how rich is His glorious inheritance in the saints (His set-apart ones).* (Ephesians 1:18 AMP)

Paul also told his followers he was letting his light shine before men by imitating Jesus Christ. Then he says, "Pattern yourselves after me [follow my example], as I imitate *and* follow Christ (the Messiah)" (1 Corinthians 11:1 AMP).

Ask Yourself...

> *Am I stopping during my day and asking myself what Jesus would do, how He would respond, and what He would say so I can let my light shine before others?*_____
>
> *Am I patterning myself after Jesus so I can tell others to imitate me?*_____
>
> *Does my character in both the good times and the tough times reflect the light of Christ in me?*_____
>
> *Are there things I need to begin to do differently so that my light shines brightly of God's love, forgiveness, grace, and mercy?*_____

If you answered no to any of the above questions, use what you learned from this lesson to begin to change what needs to be changed in your life and begin to truly let the light of Jesus Christ shine through you into the world around you and draw others to God's love.

Thank God for His great love, forgiveness, grace, and mercy in your life. Ask Him to show you how to let your light shine even brighter for Him.

Day Three: Ambassador for Christ

> *We are now Christ's ambassadors, as though God were appealing direct to you through us. As his personal representatives we say, "Make your peace with God." For God caused Christ, who himself knew nothing of sin, actually to be sin for our sakes, so that in Christ we might be made good with the goodness of God.* (2 Corinthians 5:20 PHILLIPS)

It is a great honor for us as Christians to be called to be Christ's ambassadors. According to the Merriam-Wester Dictionary, an ambassador is an official envoy; **a diplomatic agent of the highest rank** accredited to a foreign government or sovereign **as the resident representative** of his or her own government or sovereign: **an authorized representative or messenger.**[3]

To be clear though, this does not mean we are speaking for God, it means God is speaking through us concerning His **love, grace, and mercy.** Our life is to represent His message as our words and actions line up with His way of doing things.

I believe God has called me as His ambassador to those who live and work on the street. So many times they are judged and condemned by the world. I believe I am called to show them God's great love, grace, and mercy to bring them hope. When I tell them my story, they can see the truth which will set them free like it has set me free.

As an ambassador for Christ, we need to make sure the way we treat others truly reflects His unconditional love for them.

> *Never return evil for evil or insult for insult (scolding, tongue-lashing, berating), but on the contrary blessing [praying for their welfare, happiness, and protection, and truly pitying and loving them]. For know that to this you have been called, that you may yourselves inherit a blessing [from God—that you may obtain a blessing as heirs, bringing welfare and happiness and protection].* (1 Peter 3:9 AMP)

---

[3] © 2015 Merriam-Webster, Incorporated

Love

1 Corinthians 13:4-7 (NIV) describes how we are to represent God's love to others. Fill in the blanks below using this passage of scripture.

Love is _____ and _____ (verse 4).

Love does not _____, it does not _____, and is not _____ (verse 4).

Love is not _____, it is not _____, and is not easily _____ (verse 5).

Love keeps no _____ of _____ (verse 5).

Love does not delight in _____, but rejoices in _____ (verse 6).

Love always _____, always _____, always _____, and always _____ (verse 7).

Add to this 1 Corinthians 13:13 which says, these three remain: _____, hope, and _____. But the greatest of these is _____ (NIV).

Write your own definition and testimony of God's amazing love:

_____

Grace

Ephesians 4:7 says God has given each of His _____ of _____ so we can do His work.

Colossians 4:5-6 tells us to be _____ in the way we act and _____ with others especially unbelievers.

Titus 2:11 reminds us it was by God's _____ that we have been saved.

In 2 Timothy 2:1, the Apostle Paul tells us to be strong in the _____ of God.

In Acts 20:24 Paul writes that he was given the task by the Lord Jesus of testifying to the good news of _____ _____.

1 Peter 4:10 instructs each of us to use whatever _____ we have received to _____ others, as faithful stewards of _____ _____ in its various forms.

Explain God's incredible gift of grace you have received in your life:

_____

Mercy

Ephesians 2:4 reminds us of God's great love for us and how rich He is in _____.

James 2:13 says _____ triumphs over judgment.

1 Peter 1:3 tells us in His great mercy God has given us _____.

In Matthew 5:7, Jesus said, "Blessed are the _____, for they will be shown _____" (NIV).

In Luke 6:36 Jesus also tells us, "Be _____, just as your Father is _____" (NIV).

Look up the meaning of mercy in the dictionary and write it out here: _____

Describe examples of God's great mercy in your life: _____ _____

Ask Yourself...

*Is my life reflecting God's amazing love to others?*_____

*Have I given the gift of grace to others as God has given it to me?*_____

*Do I show mercy to others in the same way God has shown me His great mercy?*_____

Ask God to show you how to be an effective ambassador of His love, grace, and mercy today and every day.

Day Four: A Royal Priesthood unto God

From Jesus the Anointed, the Witness who is true and faithful, the first to emerge from death's cold womb, the chosen Ruler over all the kings and rulers of the earth. To the One who loves us and liberated us from the grip of our evil deeds through His very own blood and who established us to be His kingdom and priests for God, His Father. May glory and power be His throughout all the ages. (Revelation 1:6 VOICE)

*But you are a **chosen race, a royal priesthood**, a dedicated nation, [God's] own purchased, special people, that you may set forth the wonderful deeds and display the virtues and perfections of Him Who **called** you out of darkness into His marvelous light.* (1 Peter 2:9 AMP)

These verses just totally blew my mind. I went from the streets to the cross to becoming part of a chosen generation, a minister for God to show others His wonderful deeds in my life, and reveal the true character of the King of kings! He literally called me out of darkness into His marvelous light so I could then shine this light for others to see. I believe He chose me because if they see what He has done in my life, they will believe He can do it for them, too.

The Apostle Paul felt this way about God using him as well.

> *For I am the least of all the apostles. In fact, I'm not even worthy to be called an apostle after the way I persecuted God's church.* (1 Corinthians 15:9 NLT)

This same Paul, who had approved of the murdering of Stephen for being a bold preacher of the good news about Jesus, became a strong persecutor of all Christians. Then Paul met the living Lord on his way to arresting other Christians and his life was changed forever. Though he experienced a radical salvation, he felt he was not qualified in any way to do anything more than make tents and occasionally tell others about his conversion.

One day a man named Barnabas sought him out to go with him to help work at a church in Antioch. After that, this same Paul was sent as a missionary all over Asia Minor. He was arrested several times, had many near death experiences, and subsequently wrote most of the New Testament. His message became, "If God can use me he can use you as well," because it had nothing to do with him, it all had to do with the Christ in him.

I was amazed when I read things like this about the great Apostle Paul. Then I realized God had rescued me from a life where I was labeled as the least likely to succeed and now I have my own business and ministry to those who are labeled unlikely to amount to anything as well.

If God can take someone like me and a man like Paul and use us to help and minister to others, He can use you as well.

Ask Yourself...

> *Have I ever felt unworthy to do any significant work for the kingdom of God?*_____
> *Why have I felt that way?*_____
> *What has reading this story and these verses shown me about this?*_____

Does this mean you have to go to Bible school and study to be a priest or a pastor? A few are called to do that and serve in ministry in that way, but most of us are not. God expects most of us to serve Him by ministering to those within our immediate area of influence on a day-to-day basis.

Ask Yourself...

> *How many people that I work with do not have a personal relationship with Jesus Christ?*_____
> *How many of them need to know God's amazing love for them?*_____
> *How many of them need healing from hurts they received as children?*_____
> *How many of them feel like utter failures because of the poor choices they made in the past?*_____
> *How many are like this in my neighborhood or apartment complex?*_____

Take the time right now to start your list. Begin with the names of those you already know something about and list them in your journal and how you think you should pray for them. Then list those you have not really had enough contact with to be able to answer these questions.

Pick one name and begin to pray for God to show you a way to speak to them using your own testimony of His love, grace, and mercy in your life. Even though you may think you know what they need, be open to allow God to lead you through your conversation with them.

Remember, it is God's truth that sets you free. You do not have to force them to do anything. Share your testimony and let God work on their hearts and their minds. Just make yourself available to listen to them, and then pray with and for them if they will allow you to.

As you work your way down through your list, you will find God is using you as His "priest" to share His word and His mighty deeds so they will want to know more about the amazing God you love and serve.

Remember to record the answers to your prayers in your journal as well and add these stories to your testimony.

> *So don't be embarrassed to speak up for our Master or for me, his prisoner. Take your share of suffering for the Message along with the rest of us. We can only keep on going, after all, by the power of God, who first saved us and then called us to this holy work. We had nothing to do with it. It was all his idea, a gift prepared for us in Jesus long before we knew anything about it. But we know it now. Since the appearance of our Savior, nothing could be plainer: death defeated, life vindicated in a steady blaze of light, all through the work of Jesus.* (2 Timothy 1:8-10 MSG)

Day Five: Imitator of God

We come to God as sinners; but He wants to transform our habits, attitudes, and practices into the ways of Jesus: to live, forgive, and love as He did. So imitate God. Follow Him like adored children, and live in love as the Anointed One loved you—so much that He gave Himself as a fragrant sacrifice, pleasing God. (Ephesians 5:1-2 VOICE)

We are to imitate our heavenly Father by becoming more and more like His beloved Son, Jesus Christ. The Apostle Paul says we should tell others to imitate us just as we imitate Christ. We are to be their example of how sons of God are to behave (1 Corinthians 11:1).

Imitate the Character of God

The names of God that are used in the Bible reflect His character and show us how He wants us to act as His beloved children. Here is a list of some of those names to give you an idea of what an awesome God we strive to imitate with our lives and share about with others.

Jehovah-Jireh means the Lord our provider (Genesis 22:14). He has promised to provide all of our needs as we trust and learn to rely on Him. By doing things His way, we show others they can trust Him to be their provider as well.

Jehovah-Rapha means the Lord our healer (Exodus 15:26). One of the facets of Jesus' ministry was healing. Several places where He ministered He healed all their diseases (Matthew 9:35, 10:1; Luke 4:40). When we offer to pray for those we know are sick, we show our faith in the healing power of our God. Jesus told us this was one of the facets of our call in

Mark 16:18. I believe part of this healing includes being healed of past hurts like God is doing in my life.

Jehovah-Shalom means the Lord our peace (Judges 6:24). God offers us a peace that goes beyond what anything on this earth can give us. It is because He lifts the fear we may have lived under all our lives. His perfect love casts out fear and we need to help those around us understand this powerful truth that will set them free as well.

Jehovah-Elyon means the Lord who blesses us (Psalm 7:17). God has so much He wants to bless us with, but so many times we refuse to accept His gifts. Just as we are hurt when our children will not receive good gifts from us, we must help others understand that God only gives us good gifts that are designed to help us prosper (Romans 9:33, Psalm 37:25). Once I began to tap into these good gifts from my heavenly Father, I began to prosper and then I could help others as well. When others see how God has prospered us, they will want to become part of His kingdom as well.

Jehovah-Raah means the Lord our Shepherd (Psalm 23:1) which was one of the most powerful psalms written by a shepherd boy named David. It helps us understand a lot about our amazing God who desires to be not only our Father, but also our shepherd. Jesus explained about the role of a good shepherd in John 10:1-14. Here are some of the key verses from this portion of scripture.

Verse 3 says the sheep know the _____ of their shepherd. Verse 11 says the sheep know their shepherd will not only care for them but is willing to _____ _____ his _____ for His _____.

Verses 12-13 say that there are those who are not really good shepherds that will try to lead the sheep astray because they really ___ _____ _____ for the sheep like the true shepherd does.

In verse 14, Jesus tells us He is_____.

The point here is that Jesus leads us and trains us so we can imitate Him and become more and more like our heavenly Father. As was mentioned in a previous lesson, we should all have a mentor to guide and lead us and then we should become mentors and guides and lead others as well. However, we need the kind of servant leadership Jesus exemplified in order to truly imitate our heavenly Father.

Some of us did not have earthly fathers that gave us good role models, but our heavenly Father is the perfect role model. He even sent His Son to show us how to live the godly life on earth. Though Jesus was God's Son, He went through everything we have to go through so He could show us how to gain the victory and still maintain our godly character.

Ask Yourself...

What do I need to do to be more like my heavenly Father?

_____

How can I help others understand about our heavenly Father?

_____

Which of the above areas do I need to work on to do a better job of imitating God? _____

_____

Ask your heavenly Father to show you the areas you need to work on. Be willing to do whatever it takes to become more and more like Him. Tell God you are willing to give up friends, jobs, and even material things if it means you can become more like Him.

Day Six: A Disciple of Christ

Jesus told us all through His ministry on the earth what it was like to be one of His disciples. When we read the gospels written by the disciples in Matthew, Mark, Luke, and John, we see what it was like to walk the earth and be trained by Jesus.

We are all called to be a disciple of Jesus. A disciple is someone who is willing to be taught by the Master and then go and do what the Master has taught them to do.

Here are some of the key scriptures that will help you understand what Jesus said about being one of His disciples.

In Matthew 10:1, "Jesus called his twelve disciples to him and gave them _____ to _____ _____ impure spirits and to _____ _____ disease and sickness (NIV).

> Jesus has given this same authority to you. Explain how you have exercised this authority in your life _____
>
> _____

In Matthew 16:24, Jesus said to His disciples, "If anyone desires to be My disciple, let him deny himself [disregard, lose sight of, and forget himself and his own interests] and take up his cross and follow Me [cleave steadfastly to Me, conform wholly to My example in living and, if need be, in dying, also]" (AMP).

> Describe how you have denied yourself and disregarded your own interests to become a true disciple of Jesus _____
>
> _____
>
> In what ways have you steadfastly tried to do things the way Jesus did using His life as your example _____
>
> _____

In Luke 14:25-27, Jesus explains the Cost of Being a Disciple. He said we must be willing to give up _____ own _____.

This could mean giving up associating with friends and even some family members that might interfere or stand in the way of doing what God has called you to do.

Who is Jesus telling you to stop associating with? _____

How are they keeping you from doing what God has called you to do? _____

What plan is He asking you to change or give up in order to follow His plan for your life? _____

In John 8:31, Jesus said, "If you hold to My_____, you are really My disciples" (NIV).

How can you learn what these are? _____

Are you doing this in your life on a daily basis? _____

In John 13:35 Jesus told His disciples, "By this everyone will know that you are my disciples, if you _____ _____ _____" (NIV).

Sometimes this is one of the hardest things we have to do to be His disciple.

Are there those you are called to minister with that are difficult to work with? _____

If you want to be a true disciple of Jesus, what changes do you need to make in your attitude and behavior towards them? _____
_____

The Apostle Paul gave us a great analogy of how to work together as true disciples of Jesus.

Read Romans 12:4-8.

>This tells us we each have a _____ from God to be used
>in conjunction with the other parts of His _____.
>What gift have you been given by God to use to work together
>with the other parts of His body to benefit others and do the work
>God has sent you all to do? _____

Read 1 Corinthians 12:12-27.

>Just as the human body is made up of many parts, they all form
>_____ _____.
>If one part of the body suffers, _____.
>If one part is honored, _____.
>There should be no _____ within the body of believers
>you are called to work with.

After Jesus trained His disciples for three years He gave them their assignments. Read these passages of scripture and highlight or underline what He says we are to do as His disciples.

>*I assure you, most solemnly I tell you, if anyone steadfastly*
>*believes in Me, he will himself be able to do the things that*
>*I do; and he will do even greater things than these, because*
>*I go to the Father. And I will do [I Myself will grant] what-*
>*ever you ask in My Name [as presenting all that I Am], so*
>*that the Father may be glorified and extolled in (through)*
>*the Son. [Yes] I will grant [I Myself will do for you] what-*
>*ever you shall ask in My Name [as presenting all that I Am].*
>(John 14:12-14 AMP)

He said to them, "Go into all the world and preach the gospel to all creation. And these signs will accompany those who believe: In my name they will drive out demons; they will speak in new tongues; they will pick up snakes with their hands; and when they drink deadly poison, it will not hurt them at all; they will place their hands on sick people, and they will get well." After the Lord Jesus had spoken to them, he was taken up into heaven and he sat at the right hand of God. Then the disciples went out and preached everywhere, and the Lord worked with them and confirmed his word by the signs that accompanied it. (Mark 16:15, 17-20 NIV)

Ask Yourself...

What do I need to start doing to fulfill what Jesus has called me to do?

_____

How can I become a more effective member of the Body of Christ?

_____

*How can I help others become a disciple of Christ as well?*_____

_____

Pray and ask God to help you to become a more effective disciple of Jesus starting today.

Day Seven: A Reconciler

*For if while we were enemies we were **reconciled to God** through the death of His Son, it is much more certain, having been reconciled, that we will be saved [from the* *consequences of sin] by His life [that is, we will be saved because Christ lives today]. Not only that, but we also rejoice in God [rejoicing in His love and perfection] through our Lord Jesus Christ, through whom we **have now received and enjoy our reconciliation [with God]**.* (Romans 5:10-11 AMP emphasis added)

When Adam sinned in the Garden of Eden, he broke the relationship God wanted to have with us as His sons and daughters. Jesus came to reconcile or restore our relationship with God the Father. Jesus said, "I am the [only] Way [to God] and the [real] Truth and the [real] Life; no one comes to the Father but through Me" (John 14:6 AMP).

Begin by thanking Jesus for this great gift He has given you.

*But all these things are from God, who **reconciled us to Himself through Christ** [making us acceptable to Him] and **gave us the ministry of reconciliation** [so that by our example we might bring others to Him], that is, that God was in Christ reconciling the world to Himself, not counting people's sins against them [but canceling them]. And He has **committed to us the message of reconciliation** [that is, restoration to favor with God].* (2 Corinthians 5:18-19 AMP emphasis added)

As a disciple of Jesus and a child of God, we all have one assignment in common even though God has given us unique gifts to achieve it.

What does 2 Corinthians 5:18-19 say that assignment is?

Describe what this means to you personally? _____

_____

What are some specific ways you can begin to do this starting today?

_____

Romans 8:19 says, "For [even the whole] creation [all nature] waits eagerly for the children of God to be_____"
(Romans 8:19 AMP).

Blessed (enjoying enviable happiness, spiritually pros-perous—with life-joy and satisfaction in God's favor and salvation, regardless of their outward conditions) are the makers and maintainers of peace, for they shall be called the sons of God! (Matthew 5:9 AMP)

As children of God, our lives are to be a reflection of the blessings we receive from Him. We are to show others what a loving, wonderful God we serve.

Ask Yourself...

*Is my life a reflection of God's great love?*_____
*Why or why not?*_____
*Am I fulfilling my call to the ministry of reconciliation?*_____
*Why or why not?*_____
What changes do I need to make in my life to bring others to Him?

_____

Pray and ask your heavenly Father to continually reveal to you all that He has called you to do. Ask Him to give you the eyes to see those around you that need to hear your testimony and your message of His love. Make yourself willing to do whatever He calls you to do! You will be totally blessed if you do. I know! I am living proof!

Go to www.xulonpress.com to order this book.
You can contact the author through this email:
mistykinzel@gmail.com

CPSIA information can be obtained at www.ICGtesting.com
Printed in the USA
BVOW06s1305170216

437026BV00007B/224/P